MW01627179

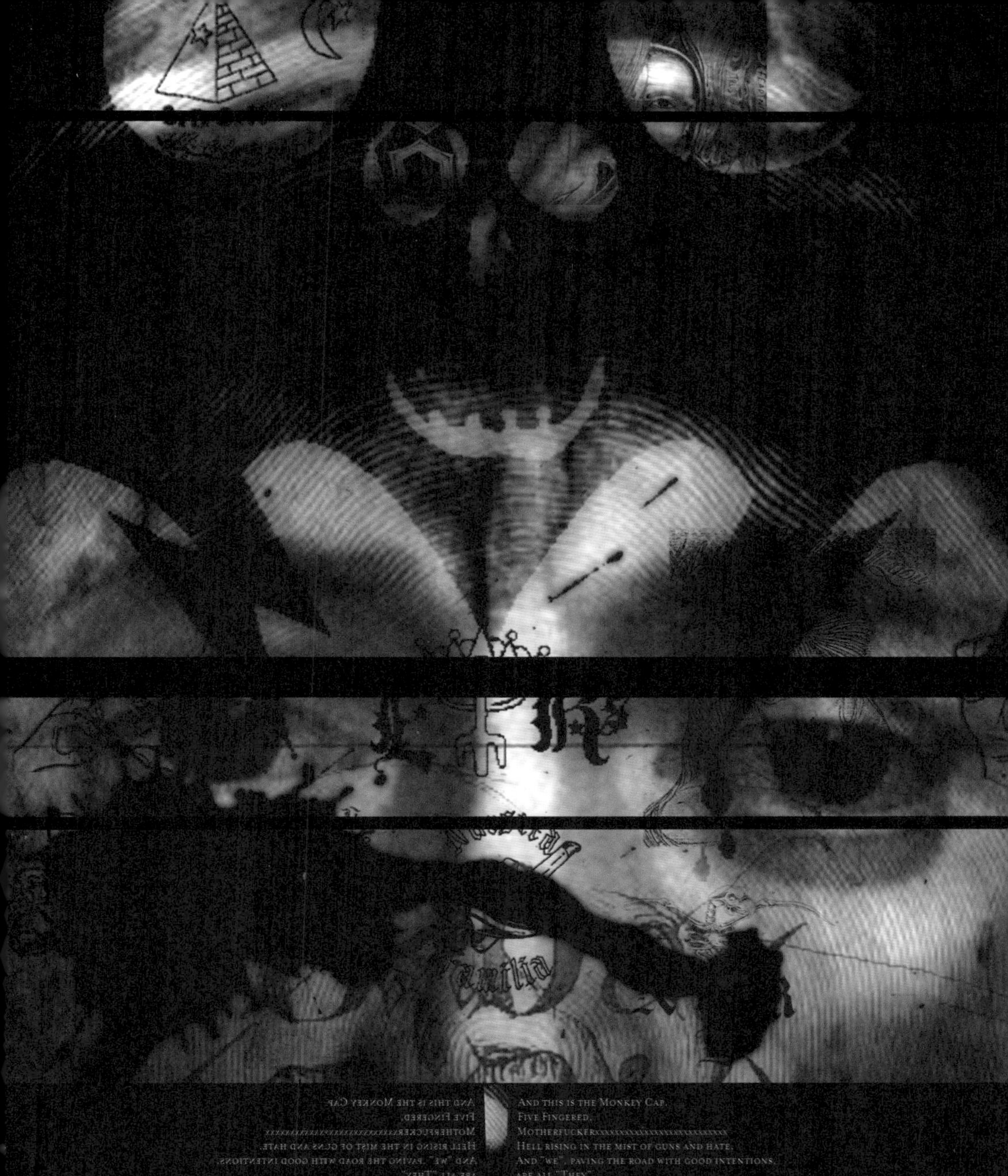

And this is the Monkey Car.
Five Fingered.
Motherfuckerxxxxxxxxxxxxxxxxxxxxxxxxxxx
Hell rising in the mist of guns and hate.
And "we", paving the road with good intentions,
are all "They".
Even you.
You, The man's keeper.
Look at it.
You live outside.
Kept books with icepicks and hollowed-points.
No different.
And those, over there, are the members with the pain in their hearts.

It's the confusion of lightning feeding our children.
Ideas of a stale-assed past.
The number 3 is creeping down the ledge.
Rock-n-Roll Mobsters. Grey faced and full of dope.

I can see clearly.

STAR
Pirate

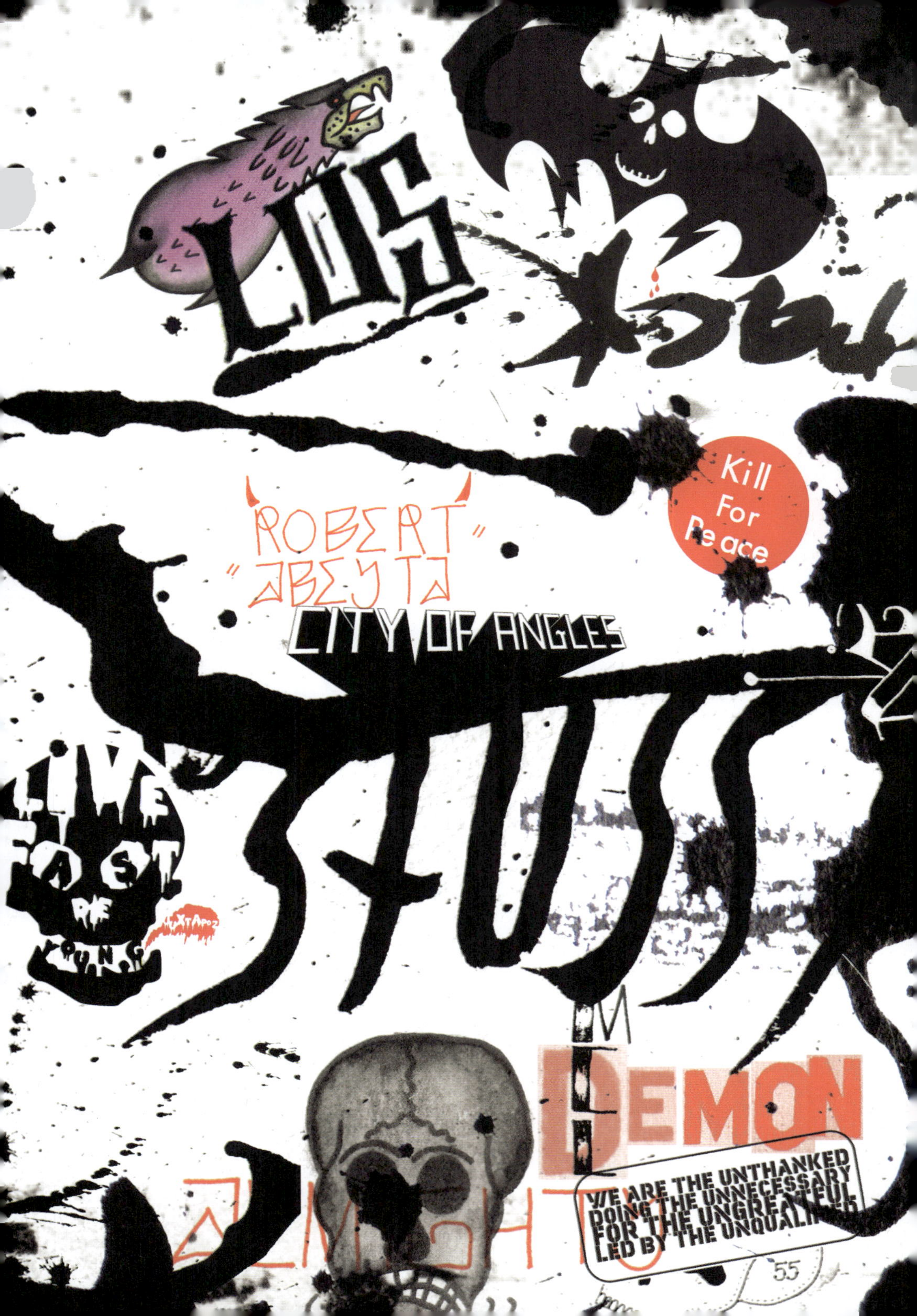
LOS
Kill
For
Peace
ROBERT
ABEYTA
CITY OF ANGLES
LIVE
FAST
DIE
YOUNG
DEMON
WE ARE THE UNTHANKED
DOING THE UNNECESSARY
FOR THE UNGREATFUL
LED BY THE UNQUALIFIED

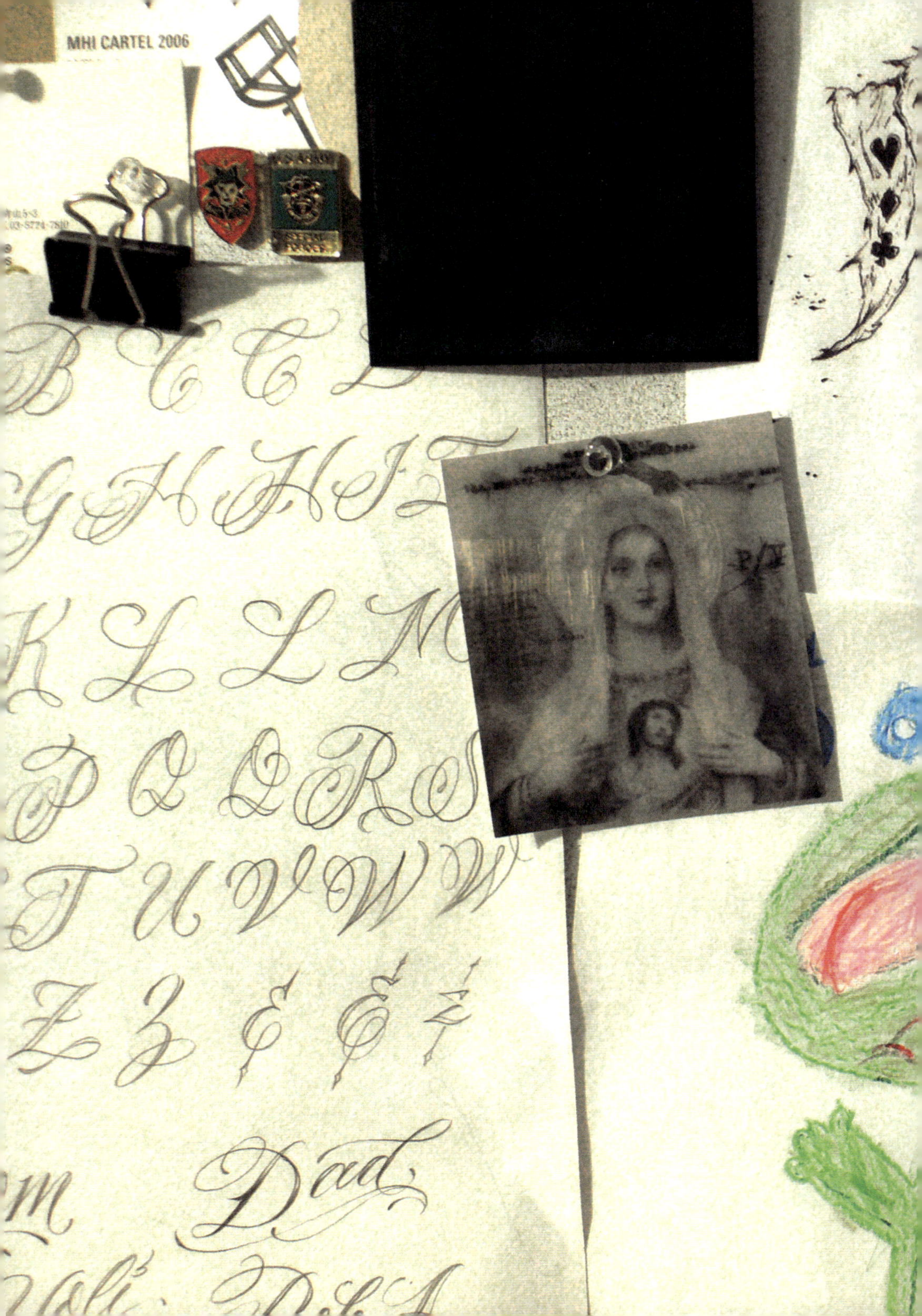
MHI CARTEL 2006
Dad

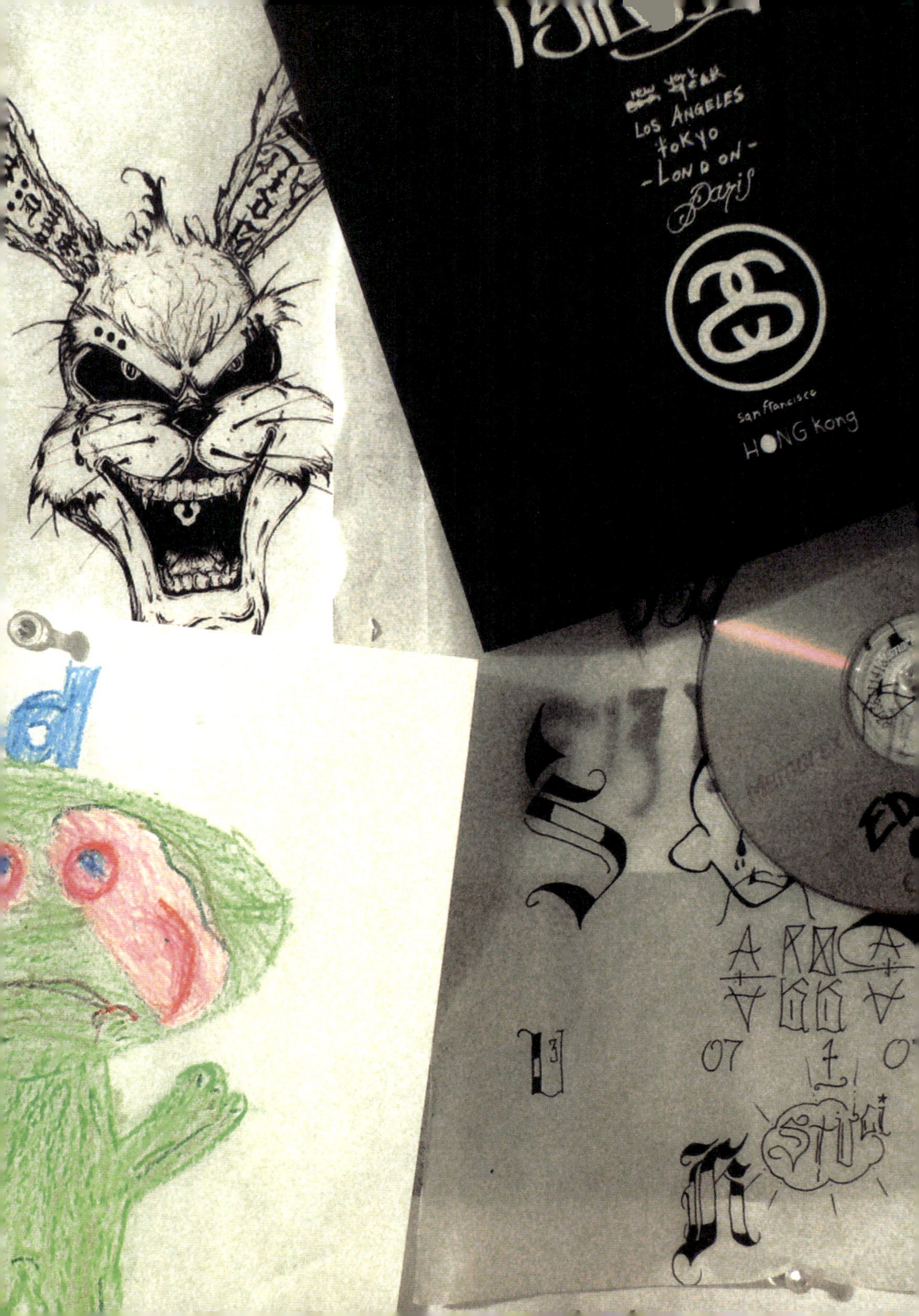

LOS ANGELES
tokyo
-LONDON-
Paris
san francisco
HONG Kong

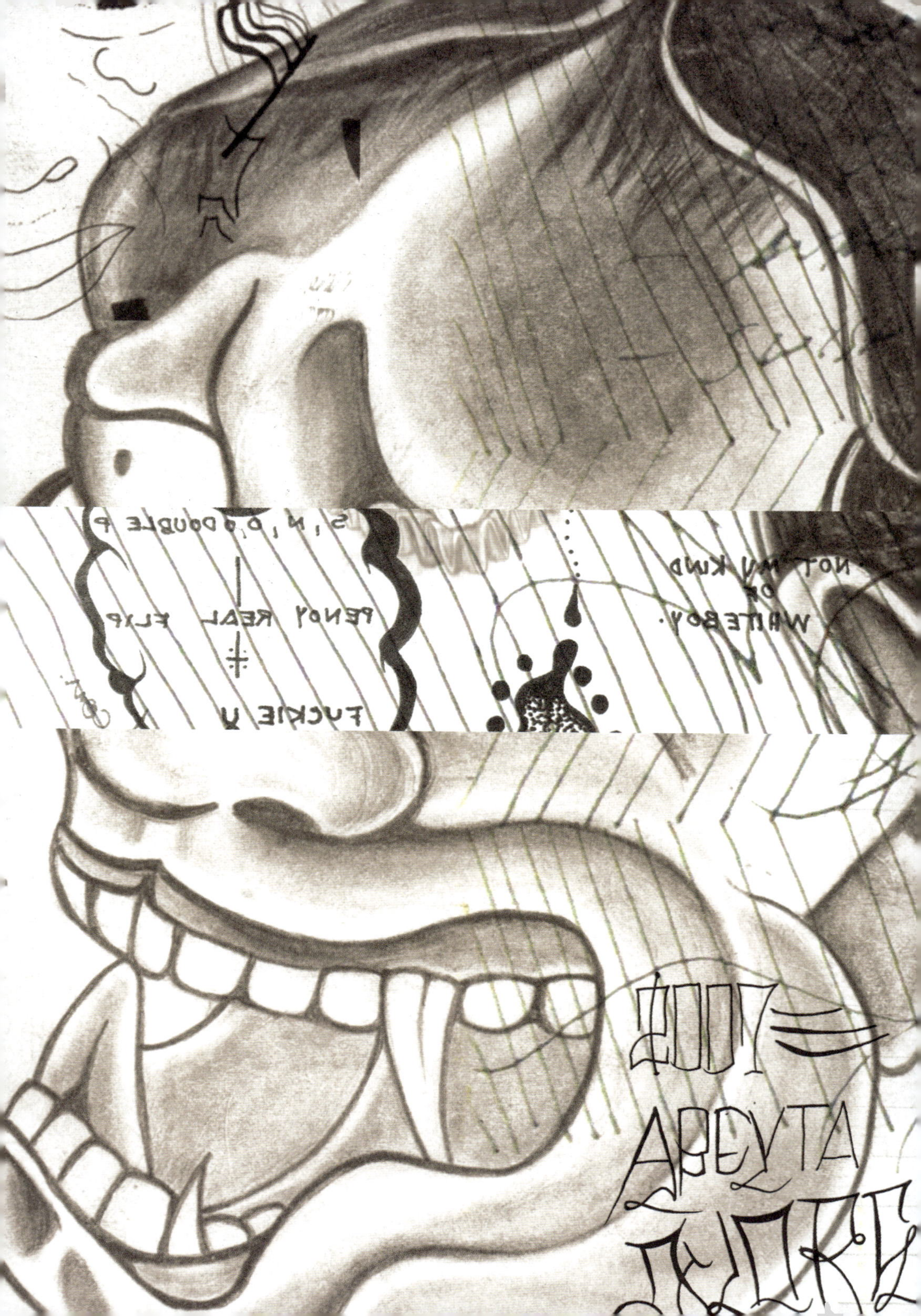

NOT MY KIND OF WHITE BOY
PENOY REAL FLIP
FUCKIE U
2007
ABEYTA

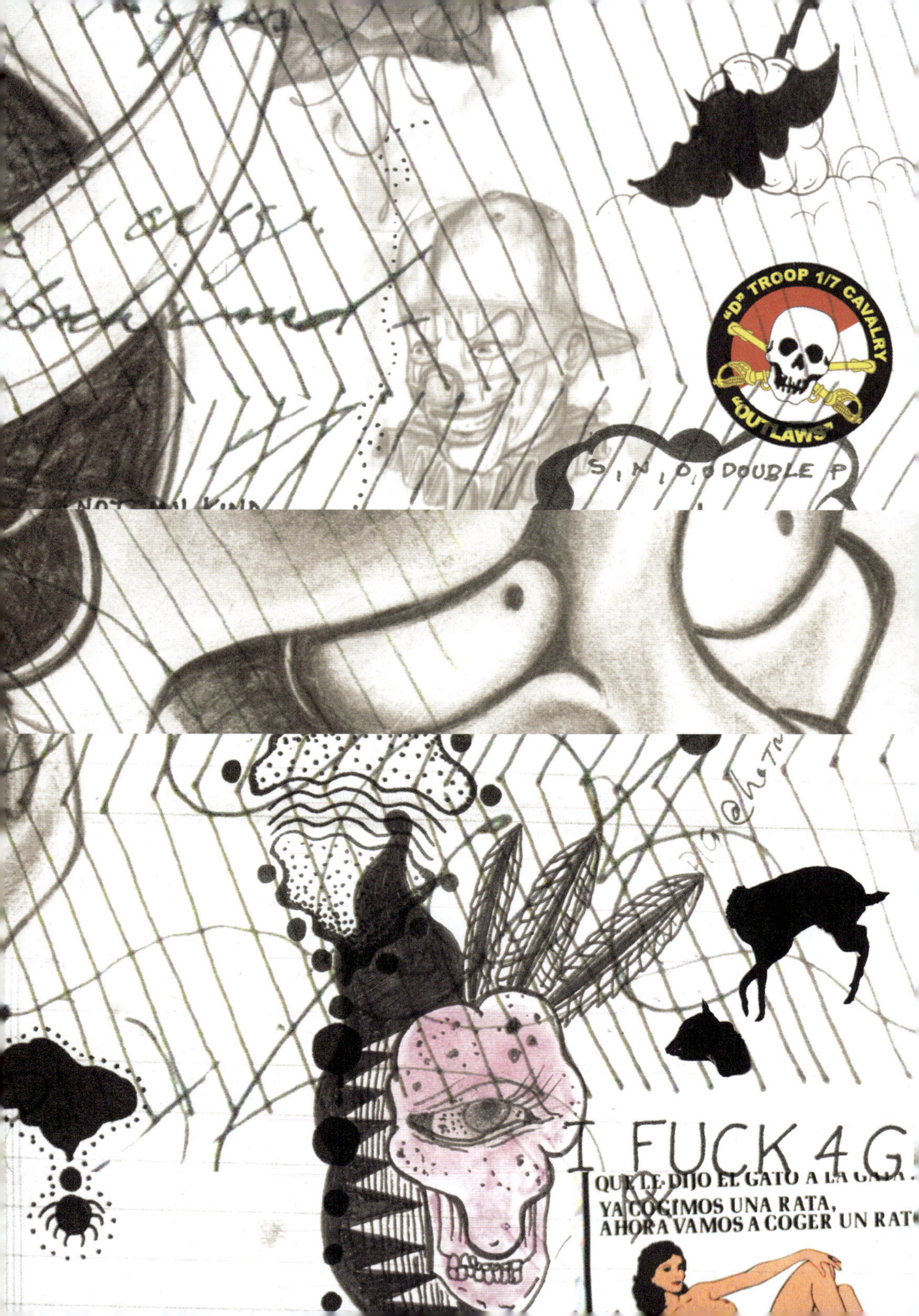
"D" TROOP 1/7 CAVALRY
"OUTLAWS"
I FUCK 4 G
QUE LE DIJO EL GATO A LA
YA COGIMOS UNA RATA,
AHORA VAMOS A COGER UN

1.
In The Car

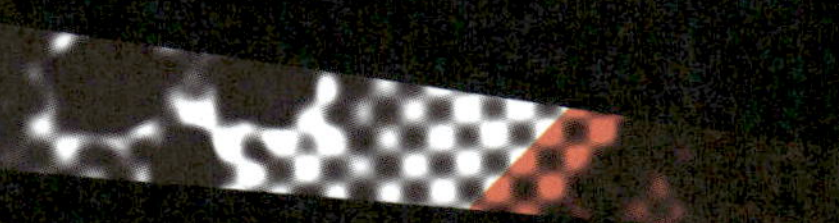

Doroteo Arango Arambula

Compliments of

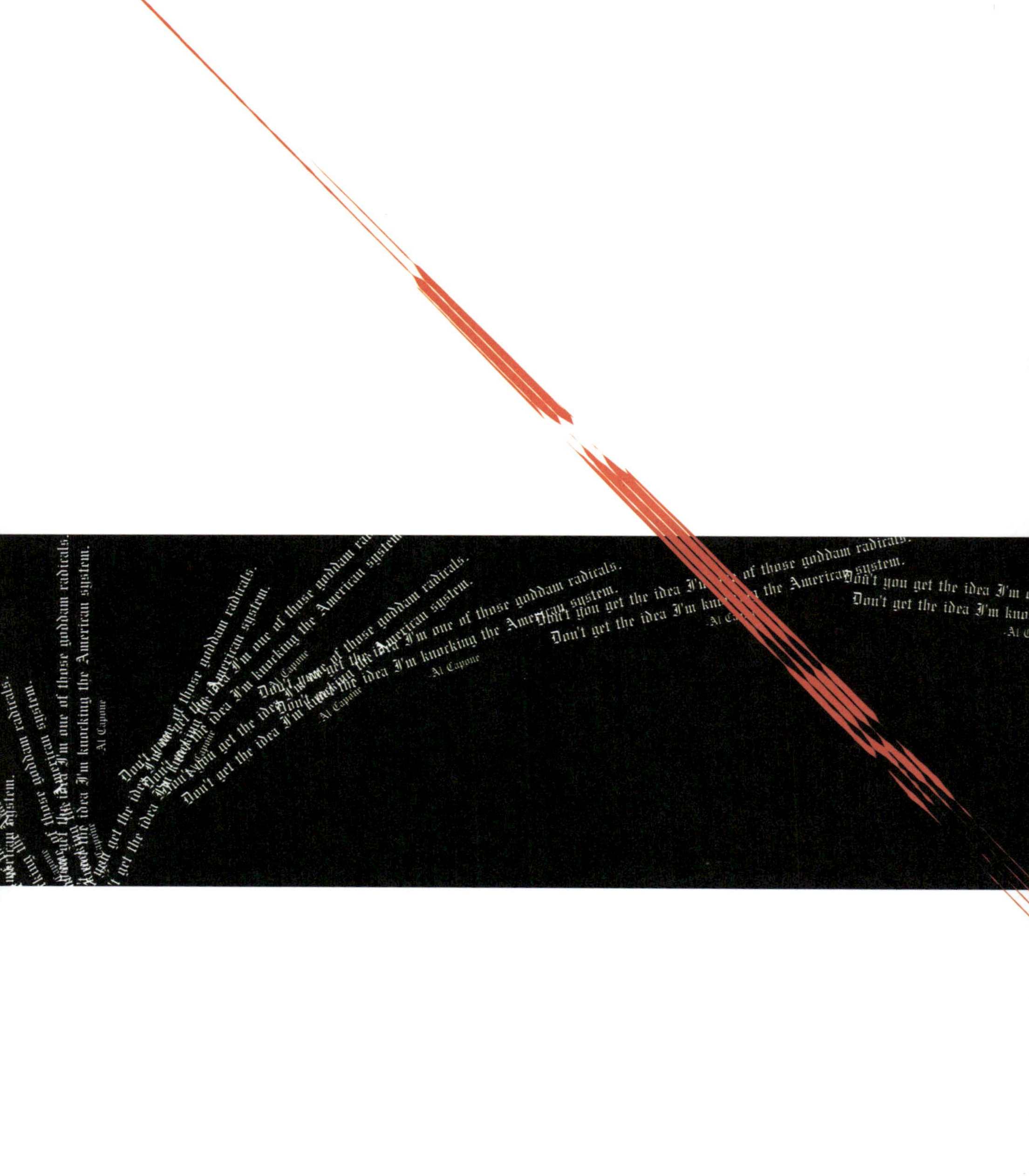
Don't you get the idea I'm one of those goddam radicals.
Don't get the idea I'm knocking the American system.
-Al Capone

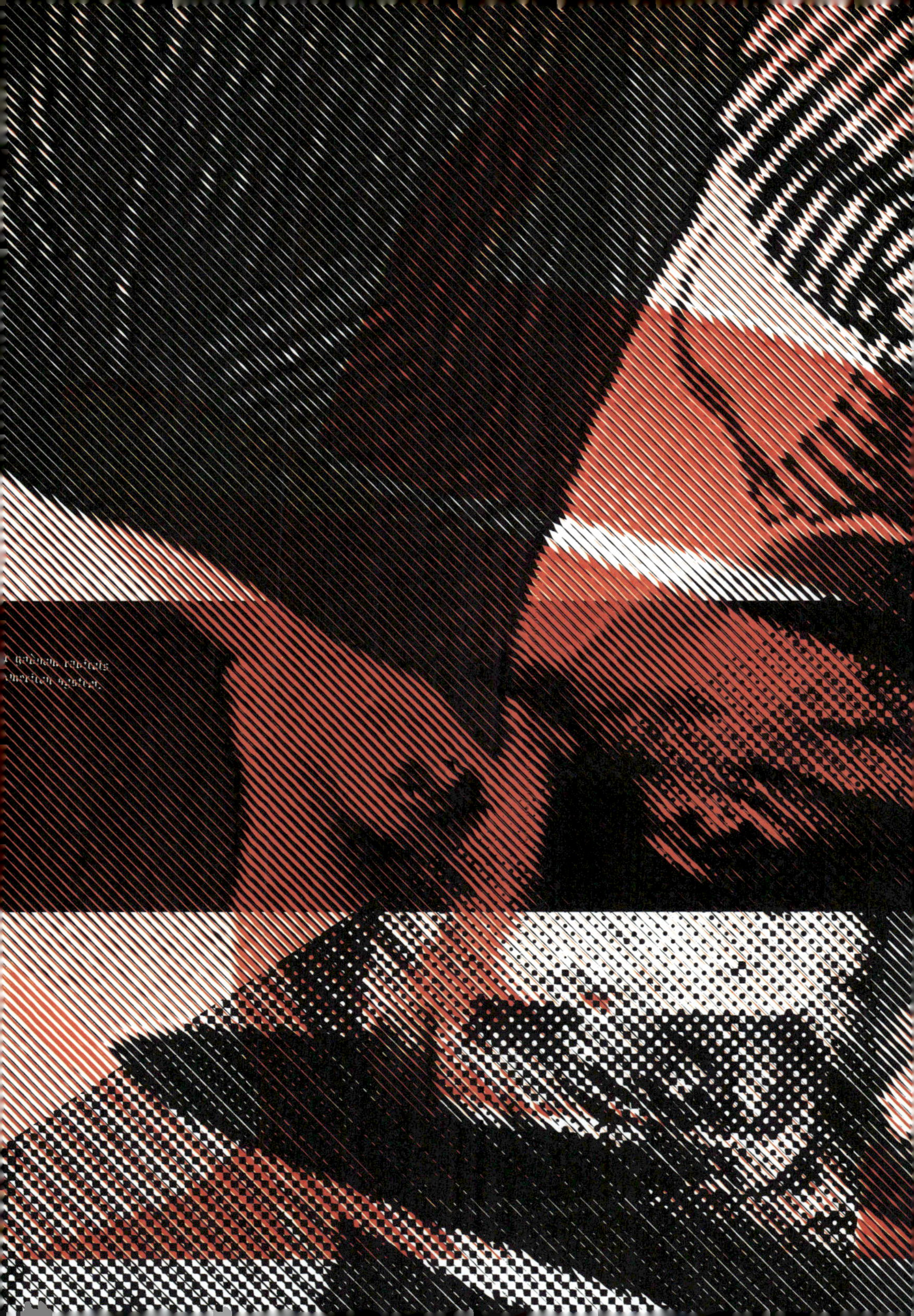

Southside

Latin Counts
Latin Disciples
Latin Kings
Queen Nation
Vicelords
Conservative Vice Lords
Blackstone Rangers
Black Disciples
The Black Gangster Disciple Nation
Simon City Royals
Two - Sixers
Latin Counts
Latin Disciples
Latin Kings
Queen Nation
Vicelords
Conservative Vice Lords
Blackstone Rangers
Black Disciples
The Black Gangster Disciple Nation
Simon City Royals
Two - Sixers
Latin Counts

Latin Kings
Queen Nation
Vicelords
Conservative Vice Lords
Blackstone Rangers
Black Disciples
Disciple Nation
Simon City Royals
Two - Sixers
Latin Counts
Latin Disciples
Latin Kings
Queen Nation
Vicelords
Conservative Vice Lor
Blackstone Rang
Black Disc
Disciple
Simon City
Two -
Conservative
Black

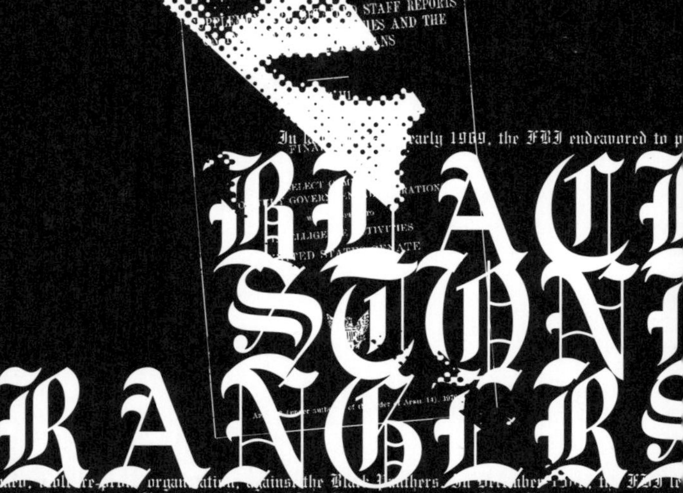

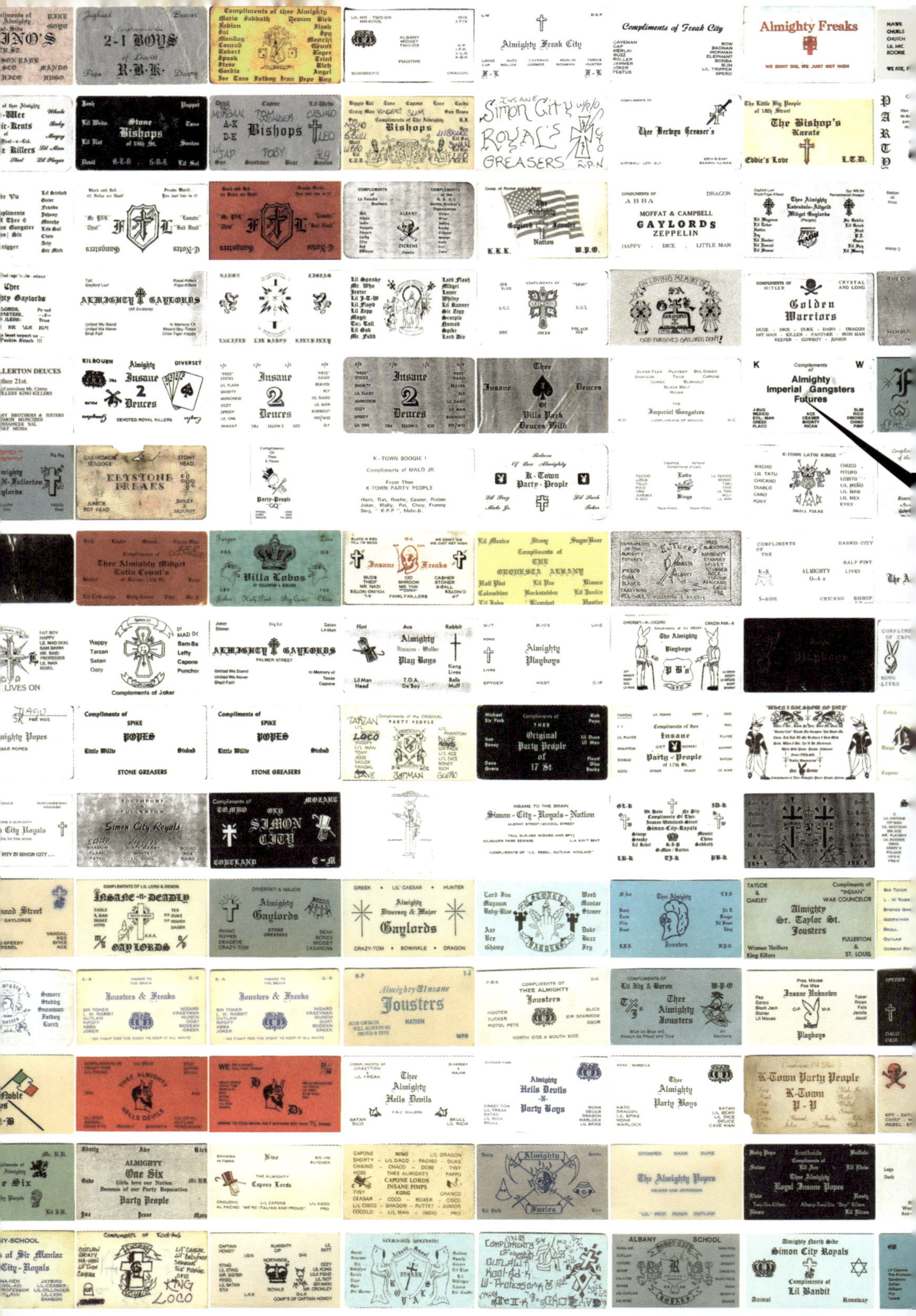

2-1 BOYS
R-B-K
Compliments of thee Almighty
Almighty Freak City
Compliments of Freak City
Almighty Freaks
WE DONT DIE, WE JUST GET HIGH
Stone Bishops
Bishops
Simon City Royal's Greasers
Thee Berwyn Greaser's
The Little Big People of 18th Street
The Bishop's Karate
Eddie's Love
L.T.D.
Gangsters
ALBANY
DICKENS
MOFFAT & CAMPBELL
GAYLORDS
ZEPPELIN
HAPPY · DICE · LITTLE MAN
ALMIGHTY GAYLORDS
United We Stand
United We Never Shall Fall
IN LOVING MEMORY OF
GOD FORGIVES GAYLORDS DON'T!
Golden Warriors
Insane 2 Deuces
DEVOTED ROYAL KILLERS
Thee Insane Deuces
Villa Park Deuces
Imperial Gangsters
Almighty Imperial Gangsters Futures
KEYSTONE FREAKS
Party-People
K-TOWN BOOGIE !
Compliments of MALO JR
From Thee
K-TOWN PARTY PEOPLE
K-Town Party-People
K-TOWN LATIN KINGS
SMALL FOLKS
Thee Almighty Midget Latin Count's
Villa Lobos
Insane Freaks
FAMILY KILLERS
ORQUESTA ALBANY
COMPLIMENTS OF THE
ALMIGHTY
CHICAGO
LIVES ON
Complements of Joker
ALMIGHTY GAYLORDS
PALMER STREET
Almighty Play Boys
Almighty Playboys
Thee Almighty Playboys
P B's
Compliments of SPIKE
POPES
STONE GREASERS
Compliments of the ORIGINAL PARTY PEOPLE
THEE Original Party People of 17 St
Insane Party-People of 17th St.
Simon City Royals
Compliments of TOMBO
OLD SIMON CITY
CORTLAND
INSANE TO THE BRAIN
Simon-City-Royals-Nation
COMPLEMENTS OF LIL LORD & DEMON
INSANE-N-DEADLY GAYLORDS
DIVERSEY & MAJOR
Almighty Gaylords
STONE GREASERS
Almighty Diversey & Major Gaylords
Thee Almighty Jousters
Almighty Sr. Taylor St. Jousters
Jousters & Freaks
"WE FIGHT FOR THE RIGHT TO KEEP IT ALL WHITE"
Almighty Insane Jousters
NATION
COMPLIMENTS OF THEE ALMIGHTY Jousters
NORTH SIDE & SOUTH SIDE
Thee Almighty Jousters
Insane Unknown
Playboys
THEE ALMIGHTY HELLS DEVILS
Thee Almighty Hells Devils
Almighty Hells Devils -N- Party Boys
Thee Almighty Party Boys
K-Town Party People
ALMIGHTY One Six
Girls love our Nation Because of our Party Reputation
Party People
THE ALMIGHTY Capone Lords
CAPONE LORDS
INSANE PIMPS
"WE'RE ITALIAN AND PROUD"
Almighty Furies
The Almighty Popes
Southside
Thee Almighty Royal Insane Popes
Simon City Royals
COMPLIMENTS OF Kool-Aid
NORTHSIDE ROYALS
ALBANY SCHOOL
Almighty North Side Simon City Royals
Compliments of Lil Bandit

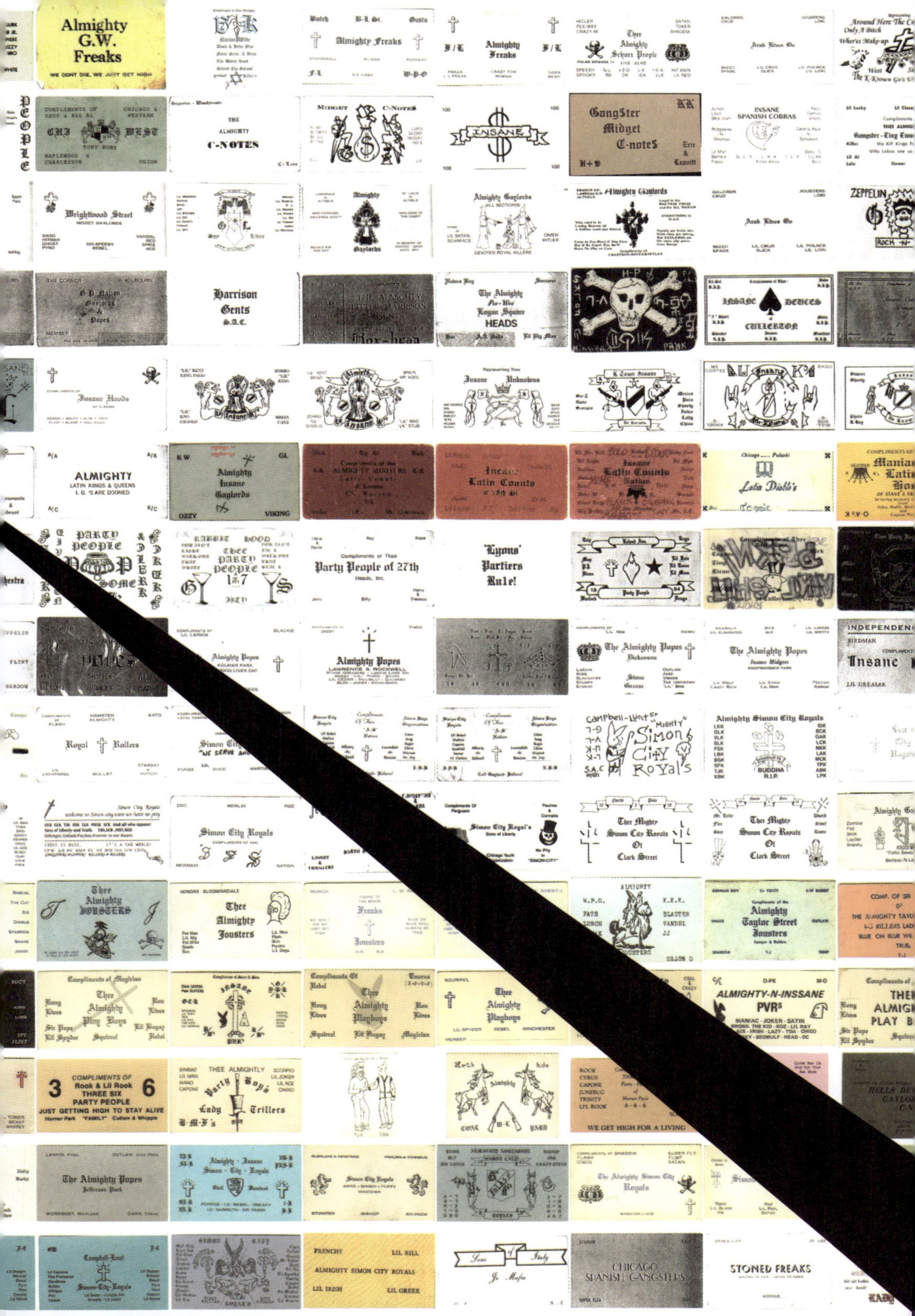
Almighty G.W. Freaks
WE DONT DIE, WE JUST GET HIGH
Almighty Freaks
Almighty Freaks
Thee Almighty Schorz People
Arab Kings On
Around Here The C... Only A Bitch Where's Make-up
COMPLIMENTS OF SKUG & BIG AL
CHICAGO & WESTERN
CHI WEST
TONY RONE
MAPLEWOOD & CHARLESTON
OHION
THE ALMIGHTY C-NOTES
MIDGET C-NOTES
INSANE
Gangster Midget C-notes
INSANE SPANISH COBRAS
ZEPPELIN
Wrightwood Street
MIDGET GAYLORDS
Almighty Gaylords
Gaylords
Almighty Gaylords
DEVOTED ROYAL KILLERS
G-P Nation Gaylords & Popes
Harrison Gents S.A.C.
THE ALMIGHTY LITTLE HARRISON GENTS
The Almighty Pee-Wee Logan Square HEADS
INSANE DEUCES
CULLERTON
Insane Hoods
Insane Unknowns
ALMIGHTY
LATIN KINGS & QUEENS
I. G. 'S ARE DOOMED
Almighty Insane Gaylords
OZZY
VIKING
Insane Latin Counts
Insane Latin Counts Nation
Latin Diablo's
PARTY PEOPLE
THEE PARTY PEOPLE
Compliments of Thee
Party People of 27th
'Lyons' Partiers Rule!
Almighty Popes
KOLMAR PARK
Almighty Popes
LAWRENCE & ROCKWELL
The Almighty Popes
The Almighty Popes
INDEPENDENCE
BIRDMAN
Insane
LIL GREASAR
Royal Rollers
Simon City
"WE SERVE AND..."
Campbell-Lunt St "MIGHTY" Simon City Royal's
Almighty Simon City Royals
BUDDHA R.I.P.
Simon City Royals
Simon City Royal's
Sons of Liberty
Thee Mighty Simon City Royals Of Clark Street
Thee Mighty Simon City Royals Of Clark Street
Thee Almighty JOUSTERS
Thee Almighty Jousters
Freaks
Jousters
Almighty Taylor Street Jousters
COMP. OF SR
THE ALMIGHTY TAYLOR KILLERS
BLUE ON BLUE WE TRUE
Compliments of Magicion
Thee Almighty Play Boys
Thee Almighty Playboys
Thee Almighty Playboys
ALMIGHTY-N-INSSANE PVR'S
MANIAC - JOKER - SATIN
Compliments of
THEE ALMIGHTY PLAY BOYS
3 COMPLIMENTS OF Rook & Lil Rook 6
THREE SIX
PARTY PEOPLE
JUST GETTING HIGH TO STAY ALIVE
THEE ALMIGHTY
Party Boys
Lady Trillers
North Side
Almighty
WE GET HIGH FOR A LIVING
HELLS DEVILS GAYLORDS
The Almighty Popes
Jefferson Park
Almighty - Insane Simon - City - Royals
Simon City Royals
The Almighty Simon City Royals
Campbell-Lunt Simon-City-Royals
FRENCHY
LIL BILL
ALMIGHTY SIMON CITY ROYALS
LIL IRISH
LIL GREEK
Sons of Italy
CHICAGO SPANISH GANGSTERS
STONED FREAKS

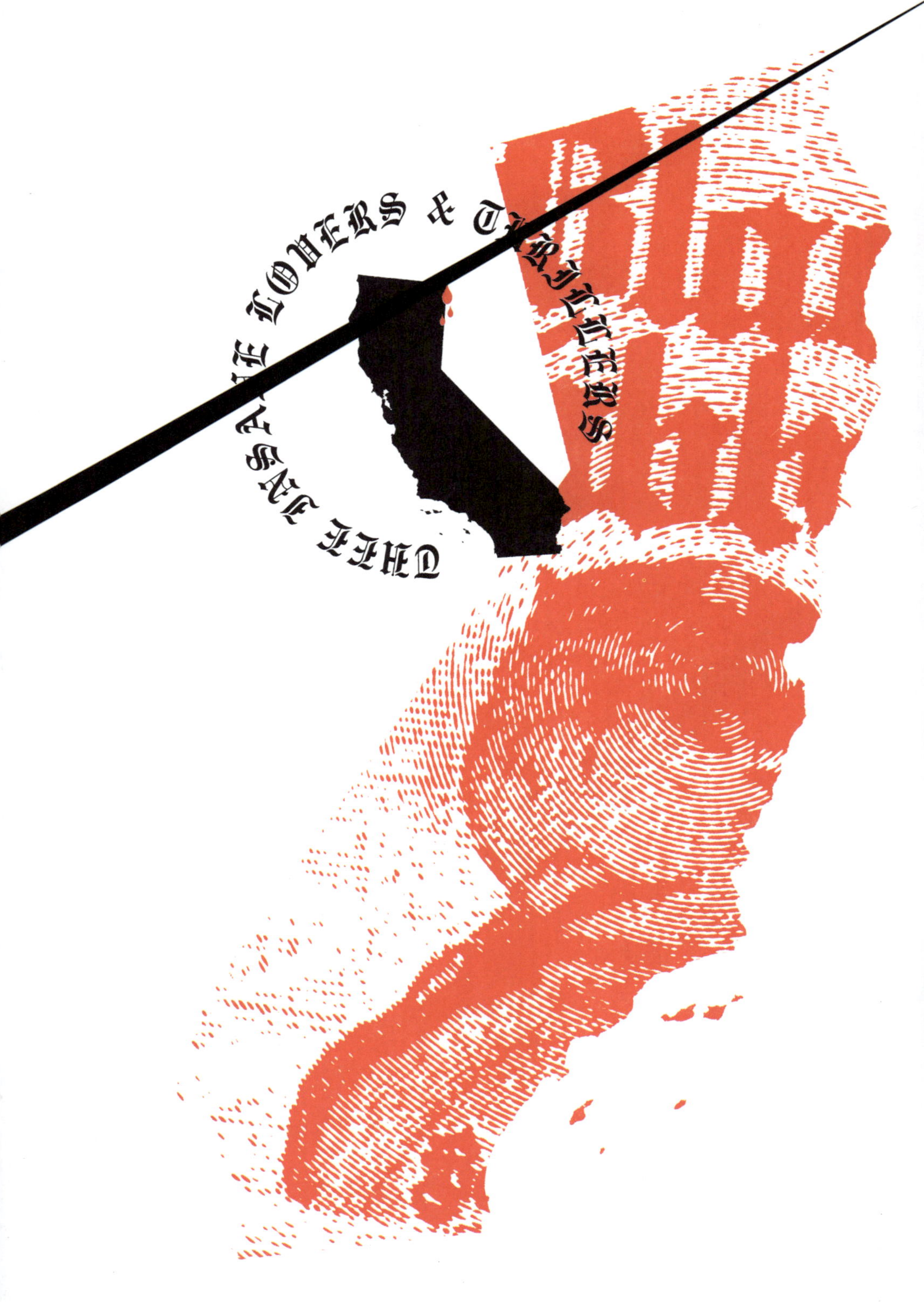

THEE
LOVERS &

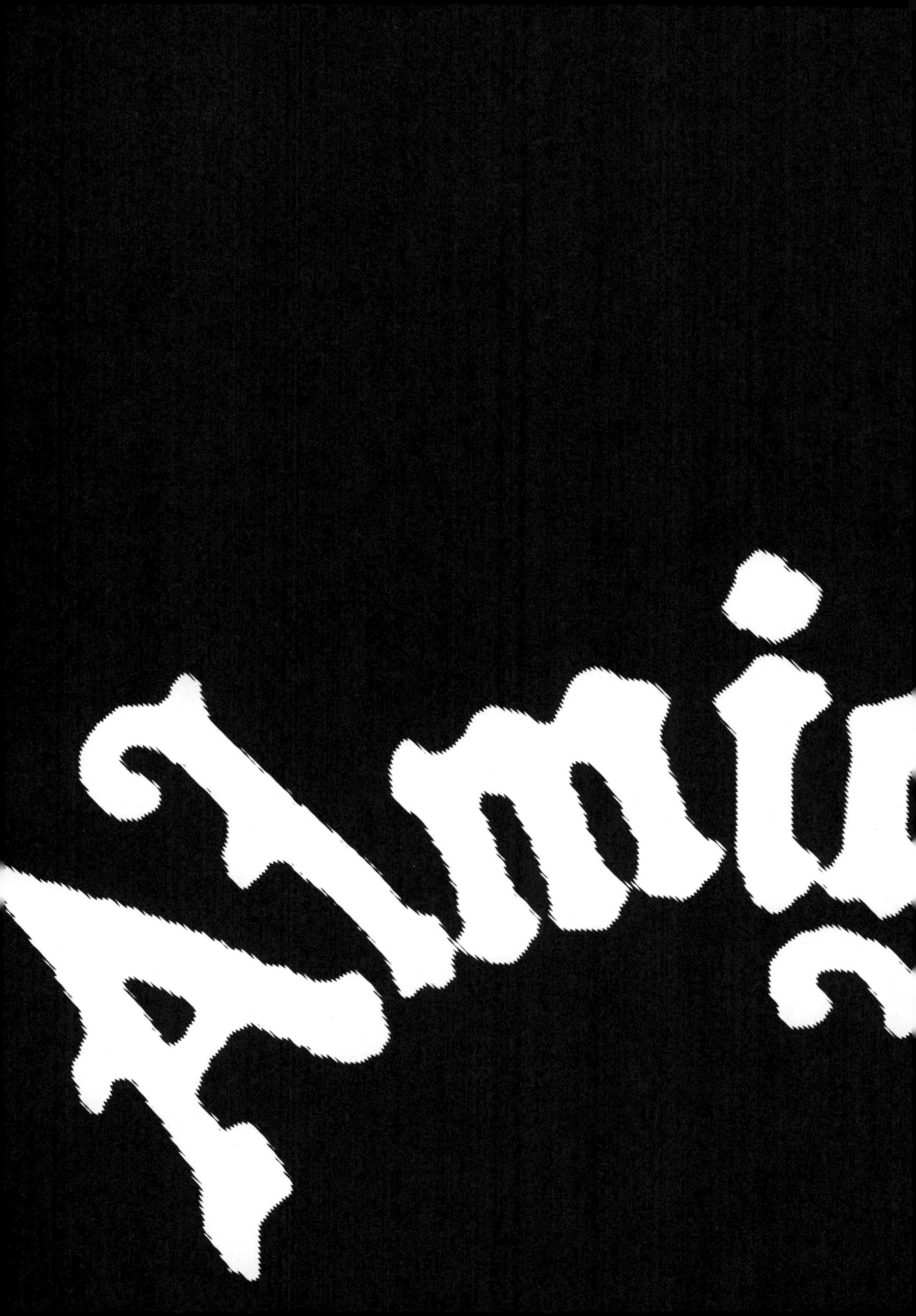
Almi

Through inter

1964

Curtis Mayfield
Sly & The Family Stone
Issac Hayes
Tower Of Power
Gil Scott-Heron

relations

were

...tional 3,000 associative relations.

...m.

Seven (7) military fragmentation hand grenades, three (3) Soviet AK-47 Assault rifles, one (1) Soviet "SKS" Assault rifle, one (1) British "Sten" Machinegun, one (1) Ruger Semi-auto carbine, several 9mm and .45 caliber pistols, and hundreds of rounds of ammunition.

THE MONEY THING IS HAPPENING AGAIN

THIS WAY THAT WAY

IT'S TEMPTING AND ALL

SOMETIMES HARD TO CONCENTRATE O

THE THINGS IN FRONT OF ME

I KEEP RUBBING MY THUMB

ON THE LEAD OF THE HOLLOWPOINT

SKIN SCRATCHES, RAW LIK

UNPOLISHED CONCRETE

NERVOUS HABIT

ALWAYS FIDGETING

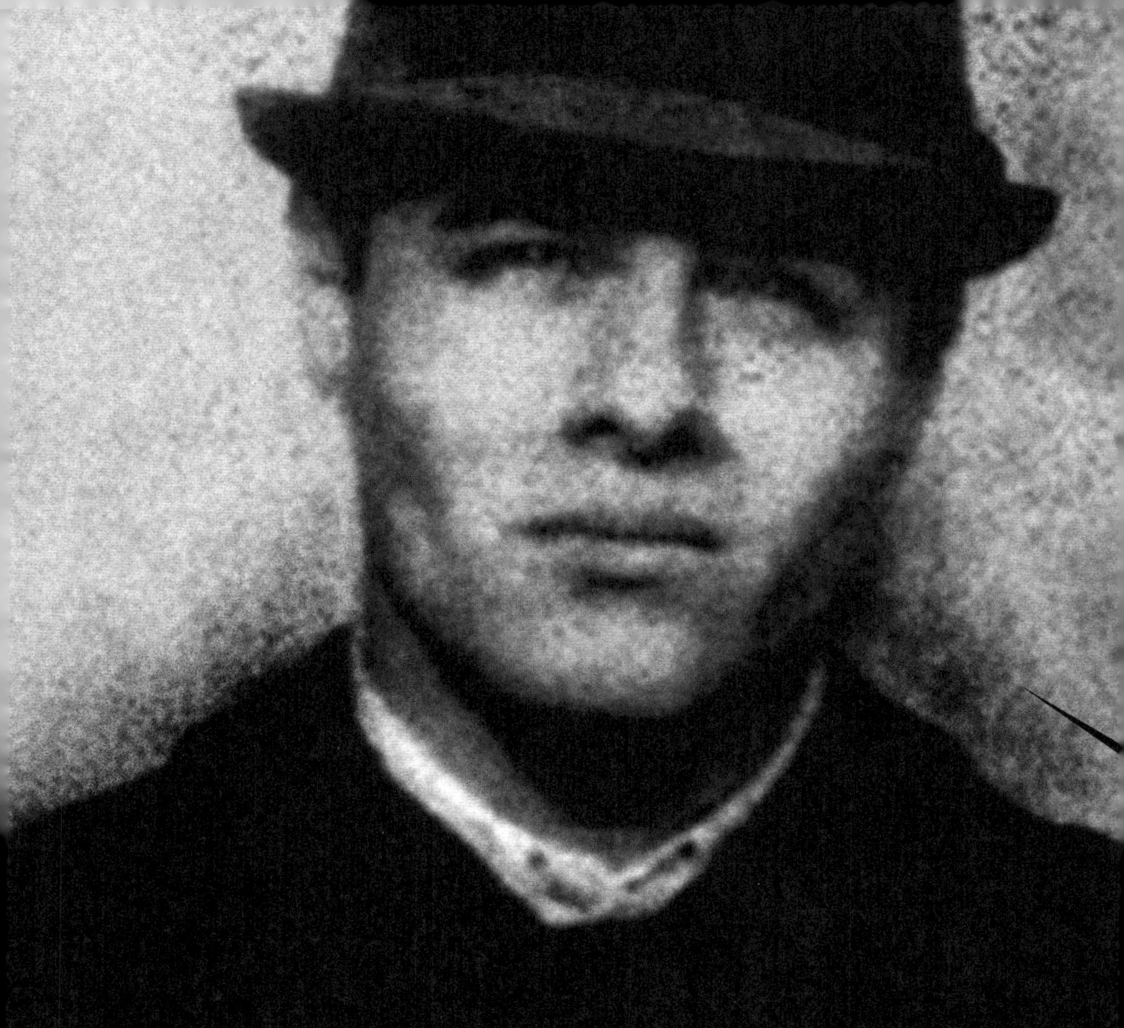
R. ABEYTA
CHI IL 5. 9.69

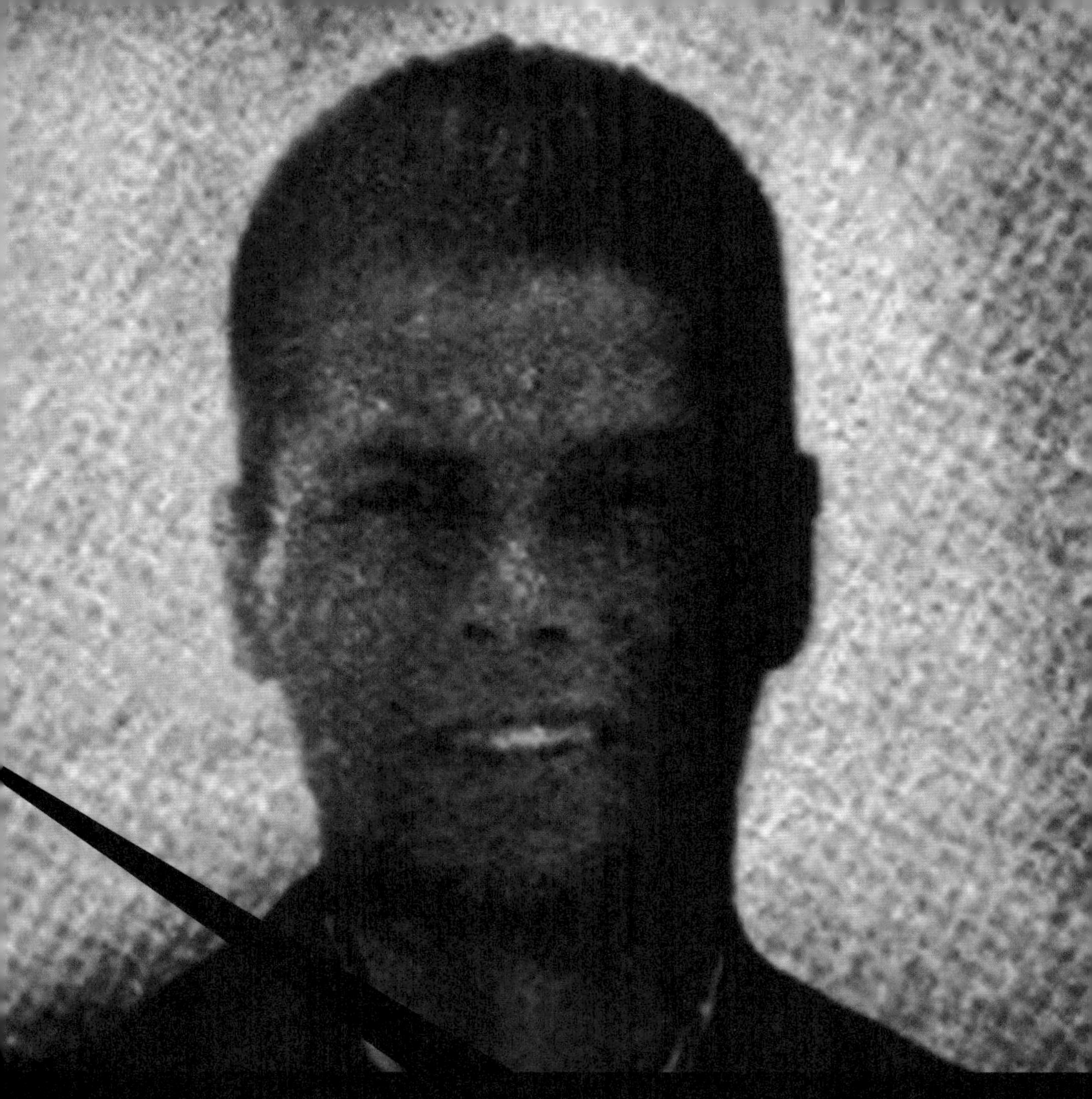

Mr. Tibbs

III.
Kill Your Parents
Passion & Aggression

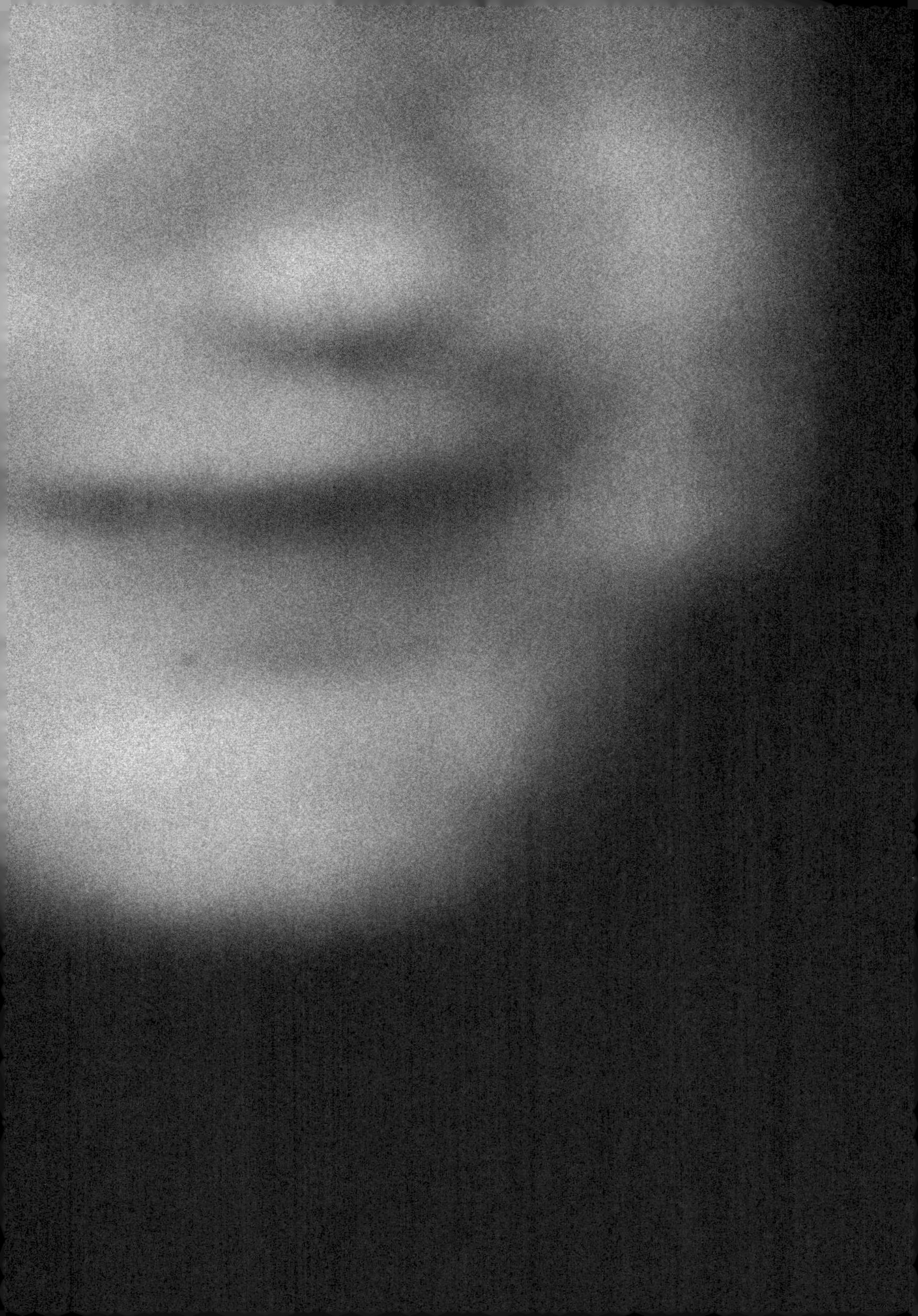

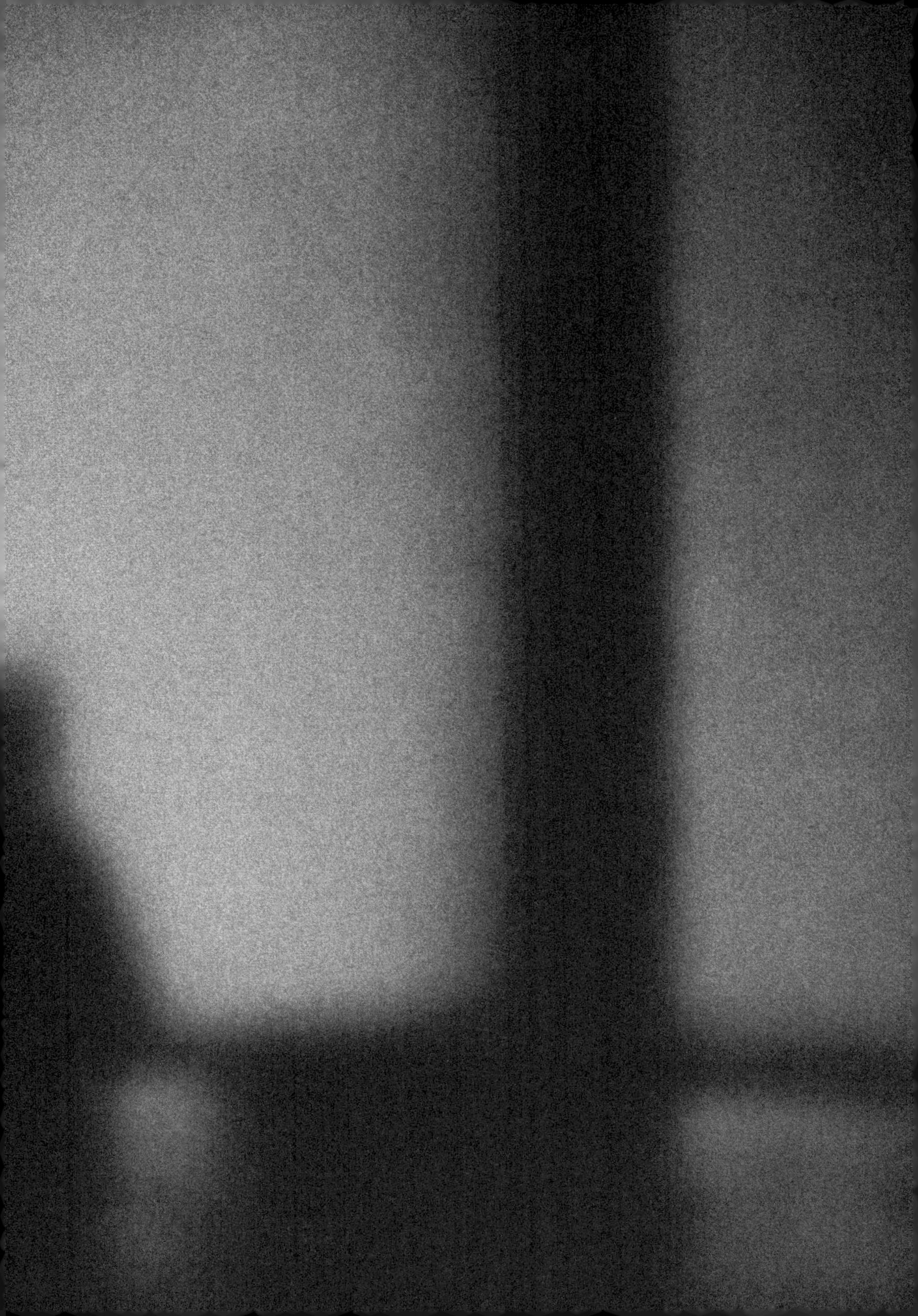

IV.
El Serio

EN EL BOTE DEL COUNTY
CON TODA MI LOCA PASIÓN
PUSE TU PLACA EN LA CEL
Y CON ESE PENSAMIENTO
ESTOY SUFRIENDO MI DESGRA

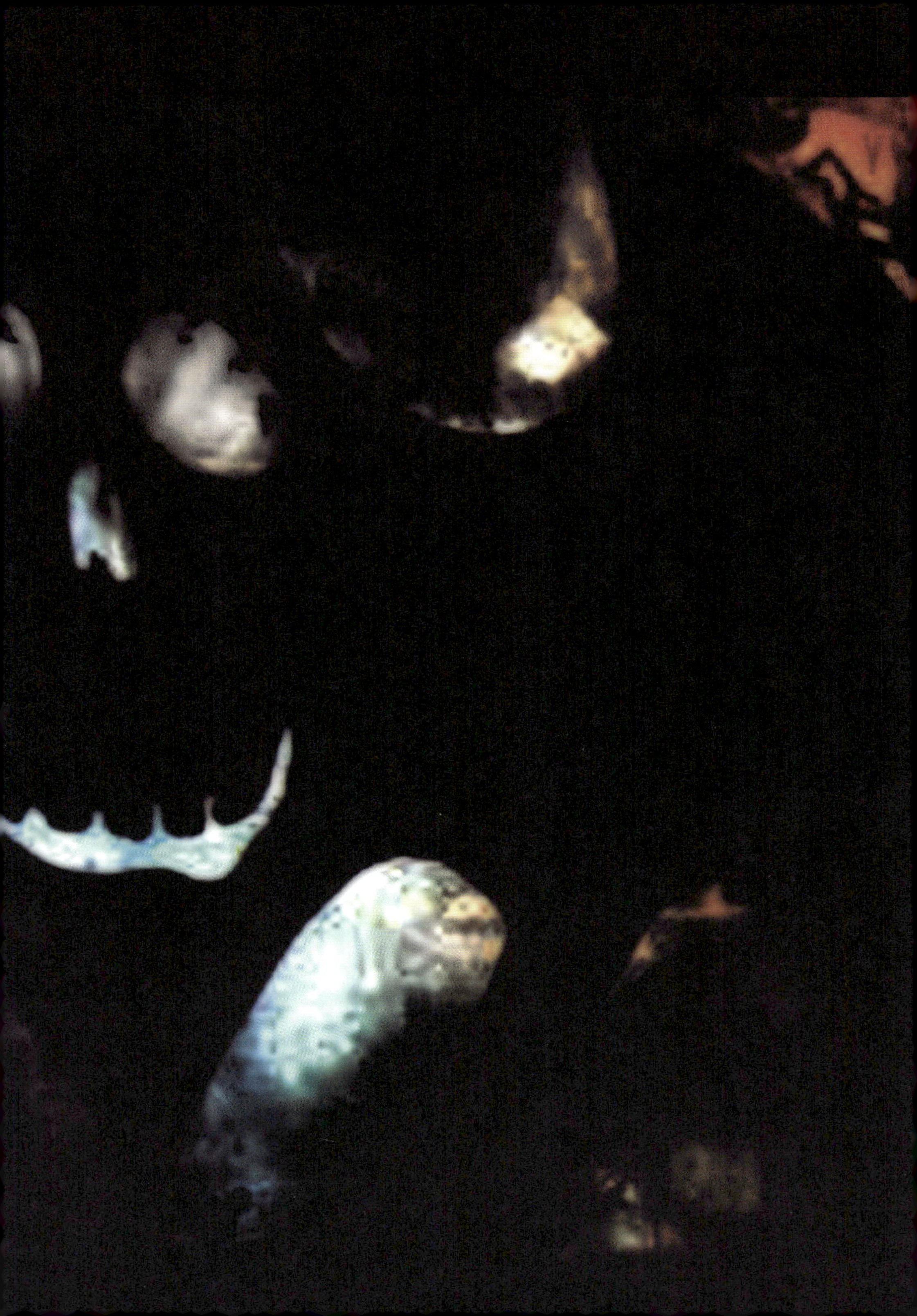

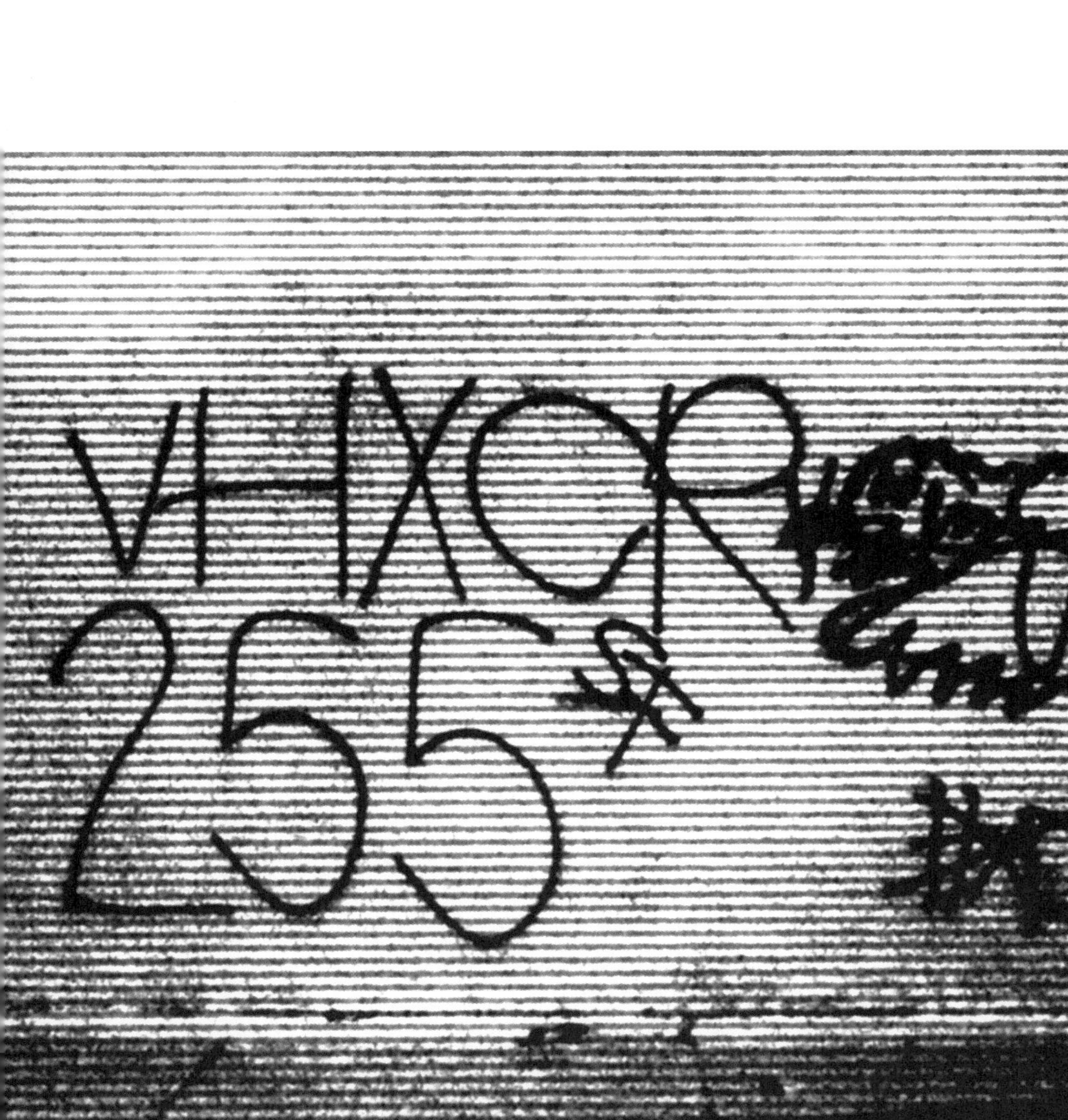
VHIXCR
255

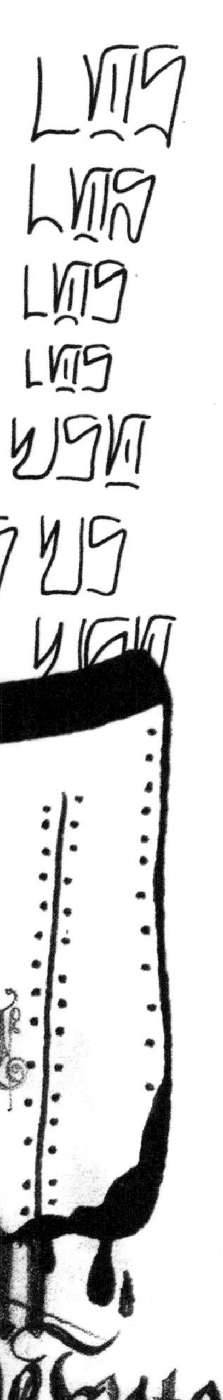

PHSXHgXmyXbHKKoHS

Two - Sixers Two - Sixers
Latin Counts Latin Counts
Latin Disciples Latin Disciples
Latin Kings Latin Kings
Queen Nation Queen Nation
Vicelords Vicelords
Conservative Vice Lords Conservative Vice Lords
Blackstone Rangers Blackstone Rangers
Black Disciples Black Disciples
Disciple Nation The Black Gangsters
Simon City Royals Simon City Royals
Two - Sixers Two - Sixers
Latin Counts Latin Counts
Latin Disciples Latin Disciples
Latin Kings Latin Kings
Queen Nation Queen Nation
Vicelords Vicelords
Conservative Vice Lords Conservative Vice Lords
Blackstone Rangers Blackstone Rangers

Curtis Mayfield
Sly
Family Stone
Isaac Hayes
Power Of Power
Scott-Heron

Through ... the ... clan grew to approximately 2,000 bl...

Compared to shootouts ... were an ocean of calm.

Dime

Zeppelin Sabbath Rock-n-Roll

Zeppelin Sabbath Rock-n-Roll

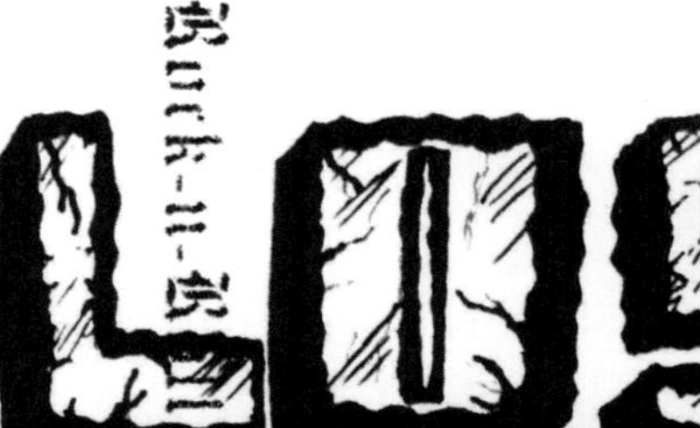

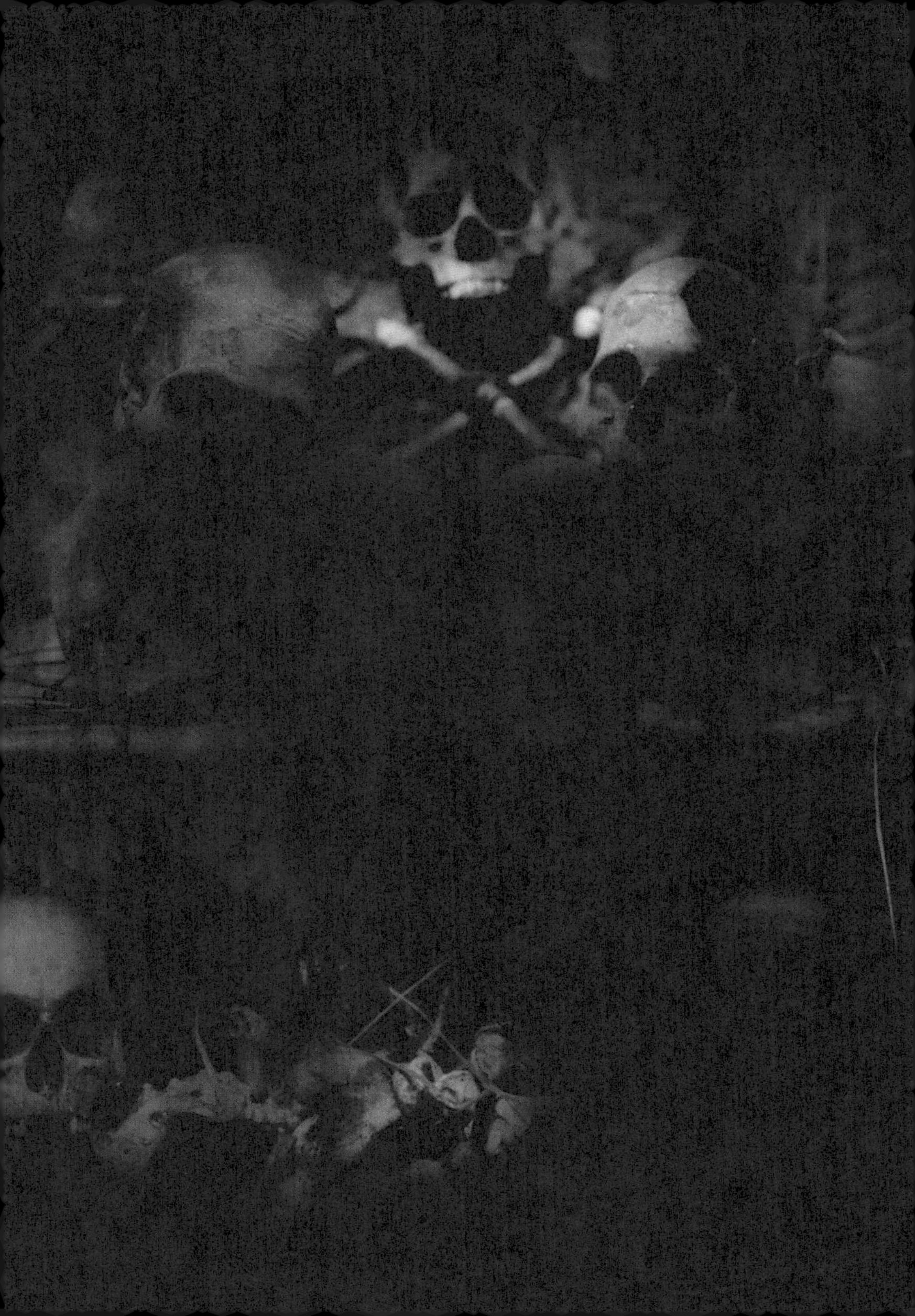

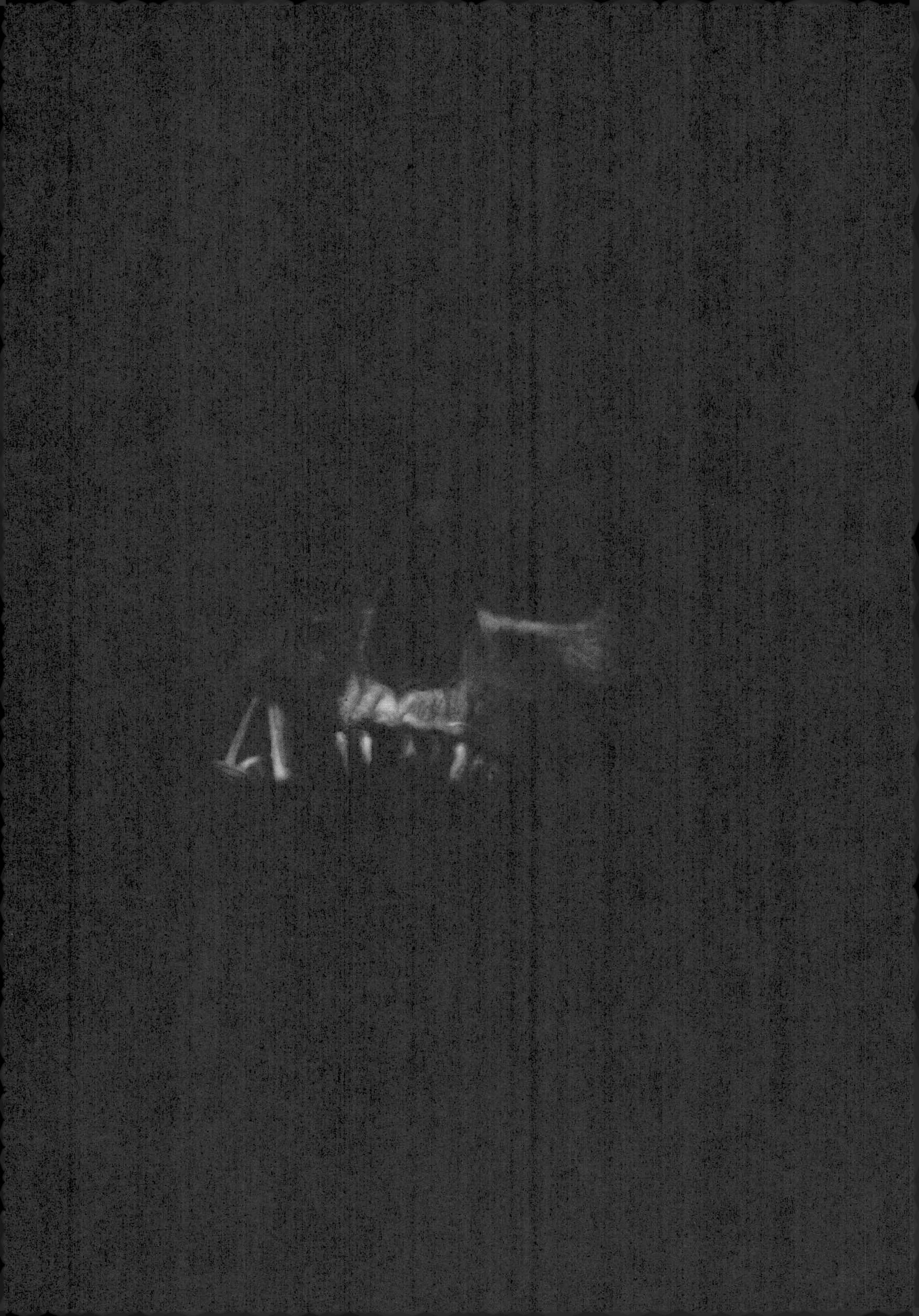

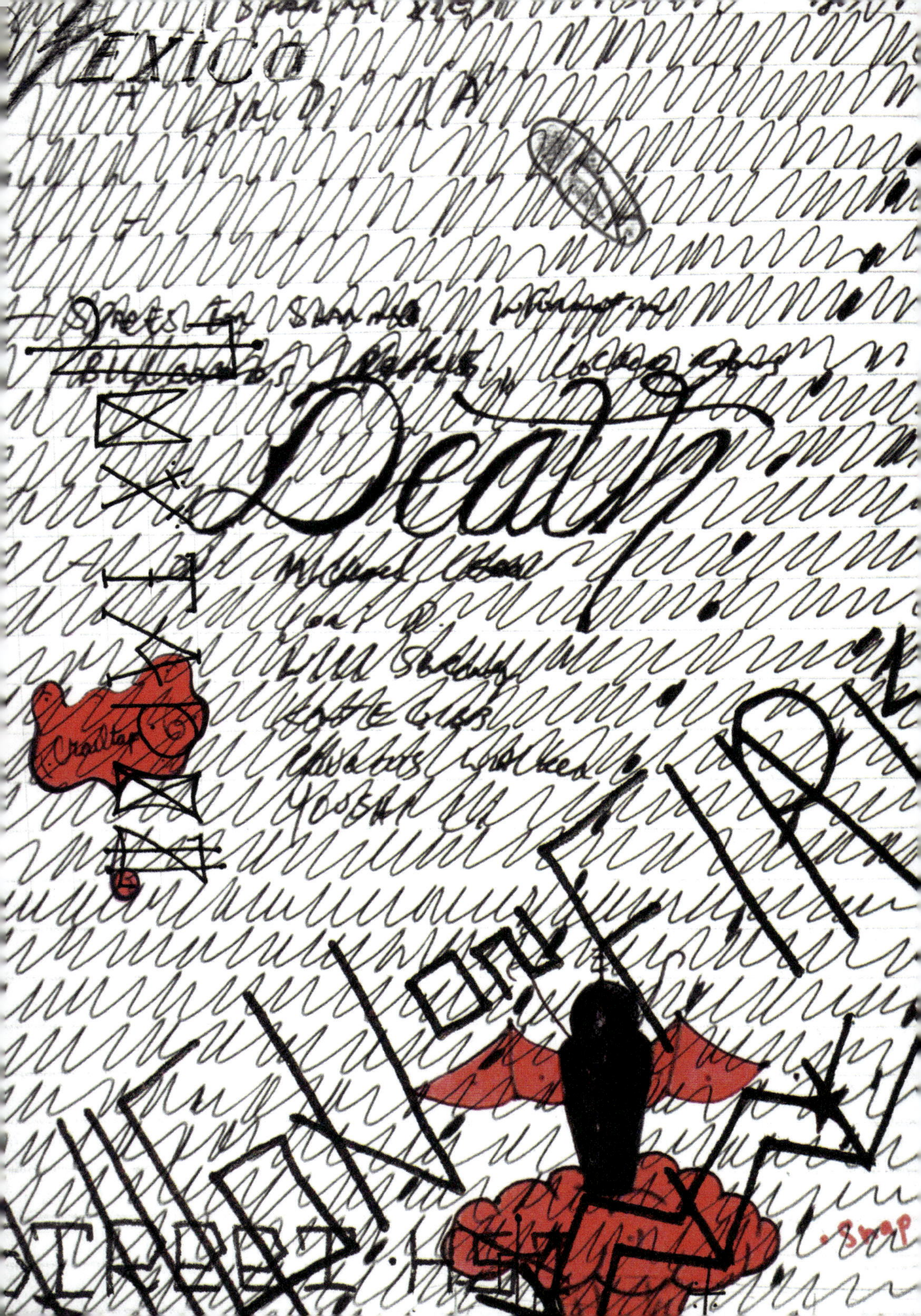
MEXICO
Death

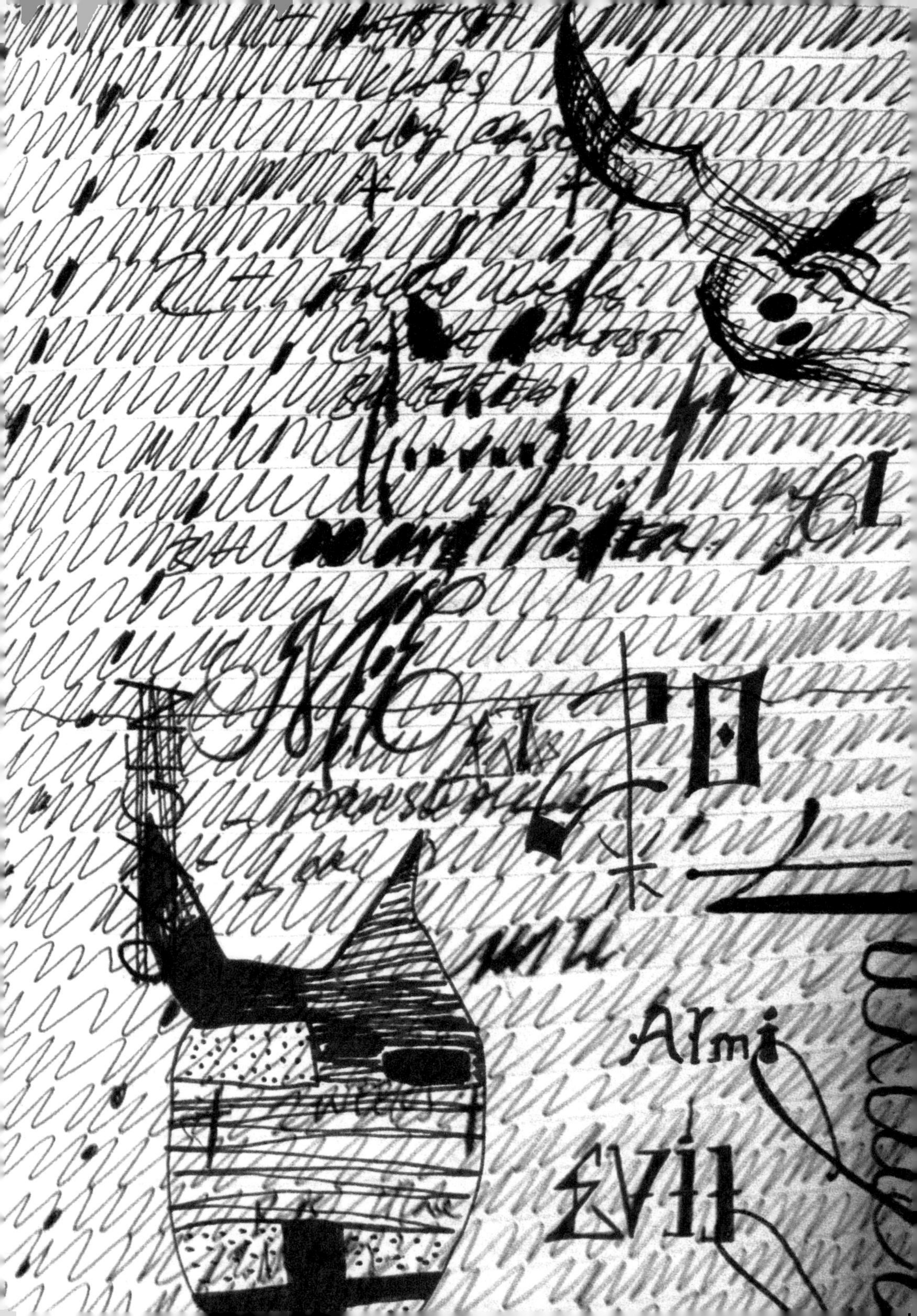
Armi

V.

The Creeping Witness

THIS CONCEPTION THAT WAS
LIEVE THAT THIS LOSER
AT HE WAS A SPIRITUAL
Middle finger

I FELT THE GREAT NEED TO TAKE A DEEP BREATH OF AIR,A GASP.
I NEEDED THE AIR ,SUSTAINER OF LIFE.WANTED TO POCKET IT ~~LATER~~
AND SAVE IT FOR LATER USE.FEAR RIPPED INTO ME,~~ONLY TO BE CORKED~~
IT WAS ME I FELT.I HATED THOSE STRANGE FEELINGS OF BEING ~~IN~~
TRAPPED IN FLESH.IT ALL SEEMED SO EXPENDABLE.
I HAD TO GET AWAY FROM DINO.GATHER MY THOUGHTS.I WAS BEGINING
TO FEEL THE DEEP REBILLION I HAD FELT IN CHURCH.CHURCH, WHERE
THEY TURN YOU INTO SOME JESUS STEAK FOR MIDDLE AMERICA TO DEVOUR
WHOLE.

I WALKED AWAY AS FAST AS I COULD WITHOUT BEING OBVIOUS I
WAS DITURBED BY THE WHOLE SITUATION.

TO FEEL THE DEEP REBILLION I HAD FELT IN CHURCH.CHURCH, WHERE
TO FEEL THE DEEP REBILLION I HAD FELT IN CHURCH.CHURCH, WHERE

THE BALL WIEGHT THING WAS SCULPTED WITH THE FINEST DETAIL,
HATS HOW GOOD I COULD SEEIT,GREAT DEATAIL LIKE A MIKE
NGELO PAINTING SAINT AND ALL.I COULD SENSE DEATH,THE WIEGHT WAS
ULLING THE BULLET IN MY GUT.TUGGING IT. SOME ONE WAS COMING TO
ET ME.I WAS GIVING UP READY TO HIT THE HIGH ROAD,WHEN
SMELLED THIS GARDEN...I SAW THIS GARDEN...IT WAS LIKE
VIGIN PURE GARDEN ..THEN ALL I REMEBER IS THE HOSPIAL."

I BEGAN TO REMEMBER READING OF SOILDERS
HAT HAD TOLD OF SIMILAR EXPERIANCES WHILE WAITING TO RECIEVE
EDICAL ATTEN[illegible] ON [illegible] BATTLE FIELD.THE PENDULLUM. THE
ODY ACUTALLY SWING[illegible] BACK AND FORTH AND THEN SMASHING INTO
SORT OF DEATH.

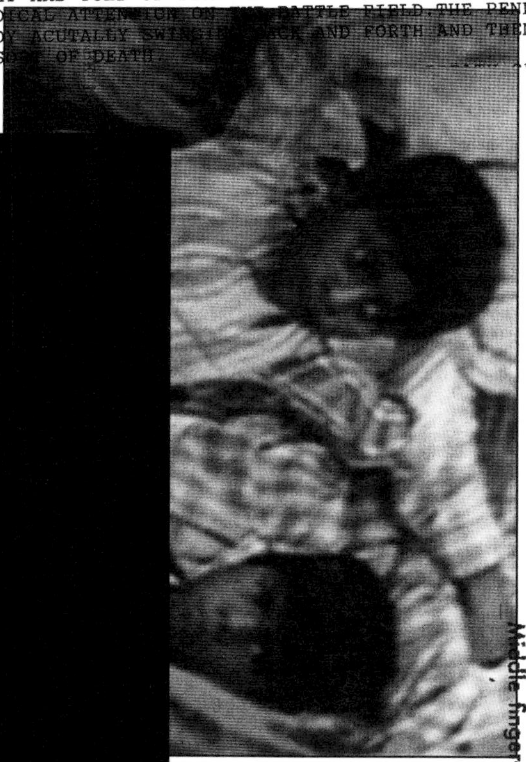

Middle finger

one of my gu

"WHAT DO YOU MEAN,..A LOVE OF LIFE...PUHH."
"JUST WHAT THE FUCK I SAID ,MAN,LOVE..L..I..F..E..."

VI.
Finger and Guns of Pure Hell

The Kid remembered
Speed Racer and the Aztec gods,
brujas and ghosts,
LA RAZA and the dance of the knife man,
the master knife man with his evil
mother who was convinced
of their white guilt.

It was just EIGHT to FIVE,
over and over again and the angels
would never come.
Just BRUJAS with friendly smiles and
STINKY EYE.

We painted our windows with blueish green and
threw magical pentagrams for saftey.

They still would come to our house.

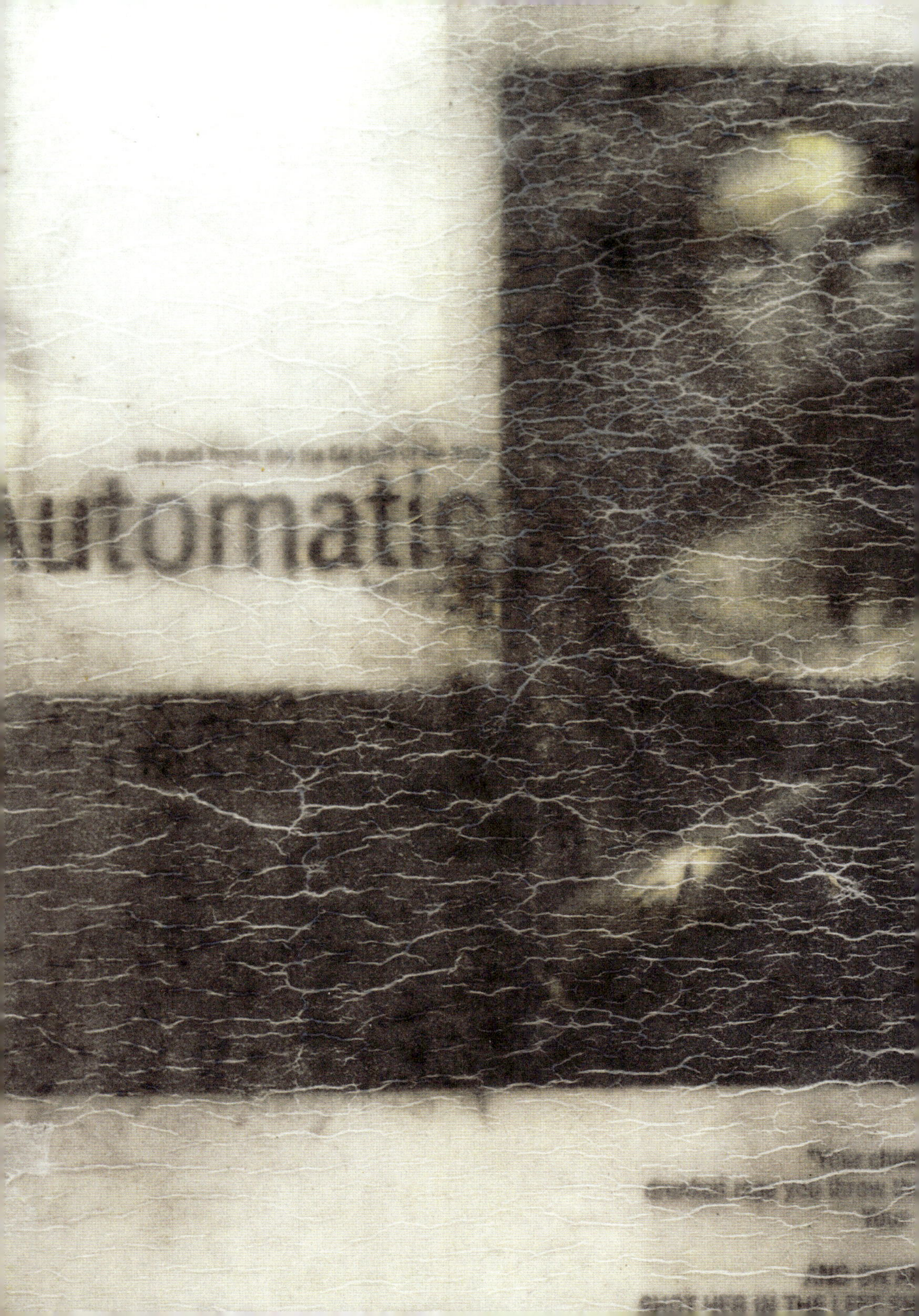
utomati

"Look man,I ain"t looking for no power trip or anything...
I'm just looking to make some money so I can have the Ameri
Dream.You know how much a house goes for these days?
Six digits,Bro...~~man~~, I was at the Rameriz Bros. house,
they told me I ~~too~~ could own a house like theirs.

STINKY EYED, red pursed lips, weathered brown skin... they spoke of hate and race, color and creed, classification, subjugation.

They pounded the morality of prison and armored truck robbery into The Kid.

Thru retail drug sales, gangs and drive-bys, militias and skinheads, they planned the last lick of the land with the politicians,
the ulta-rich capitalists, and the self-hating.

"Use fertilizer, crack, pins and needles, heroin and speed, bullets and knives and explain to the children its all part of life."

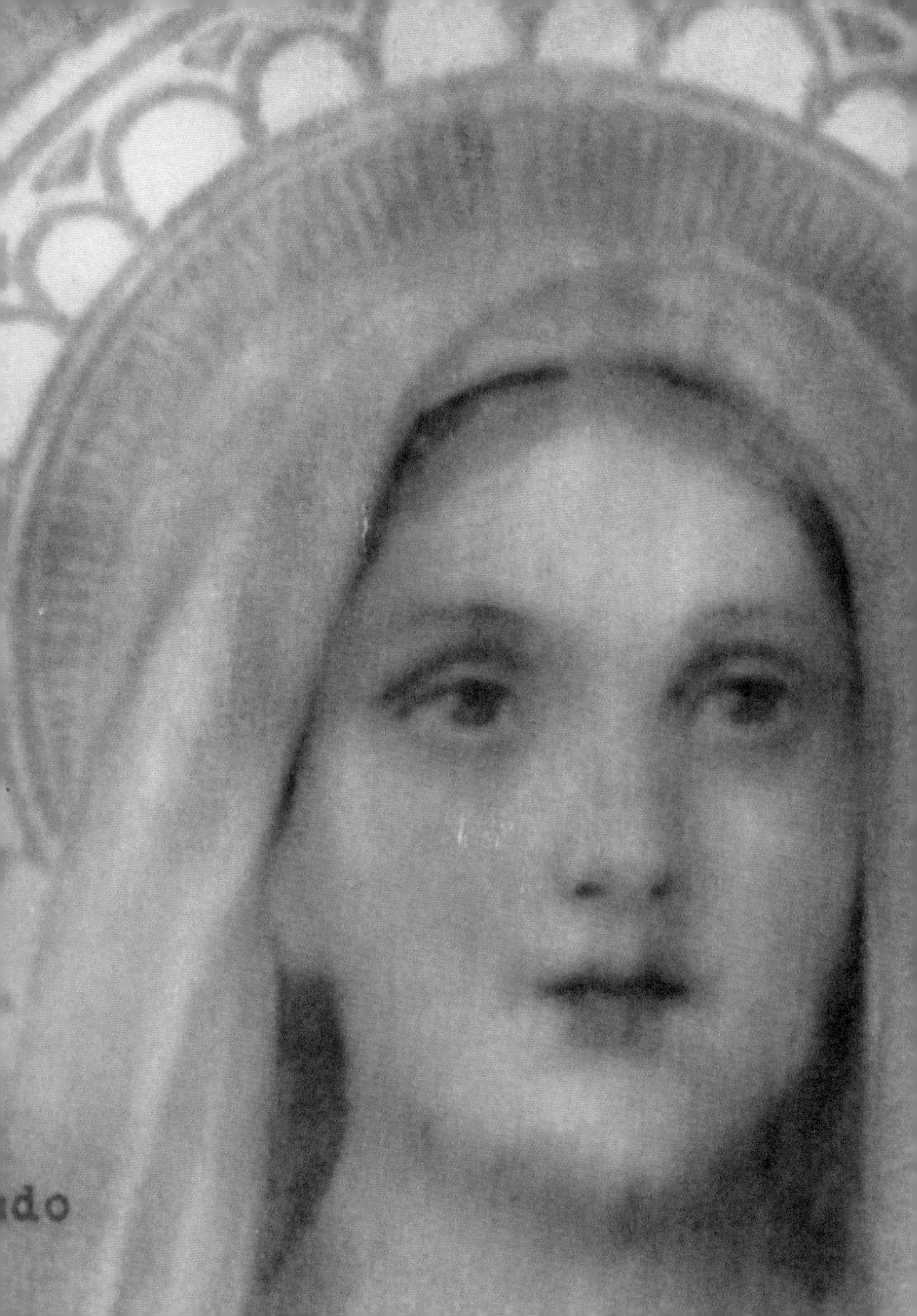

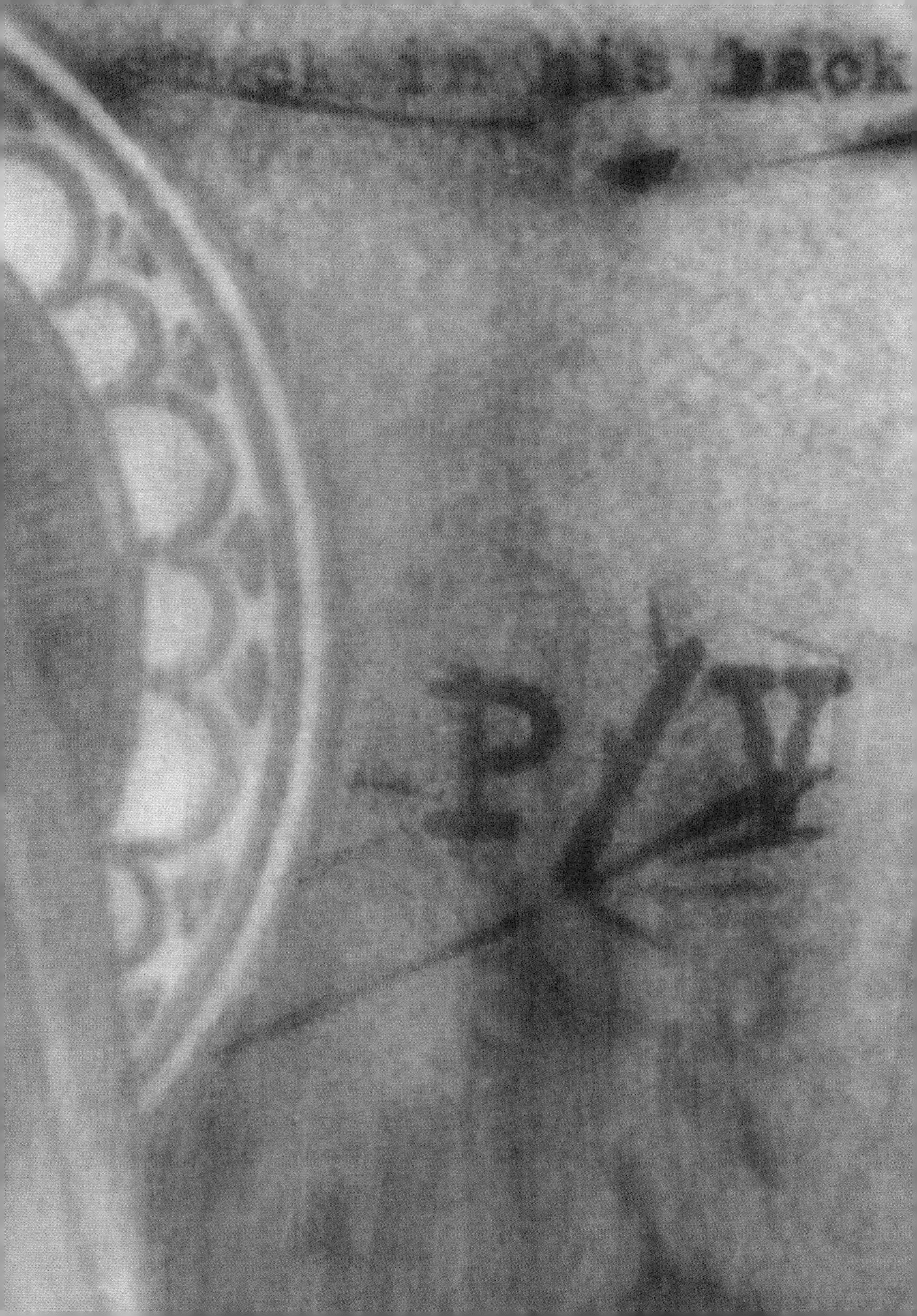
in his back
P V

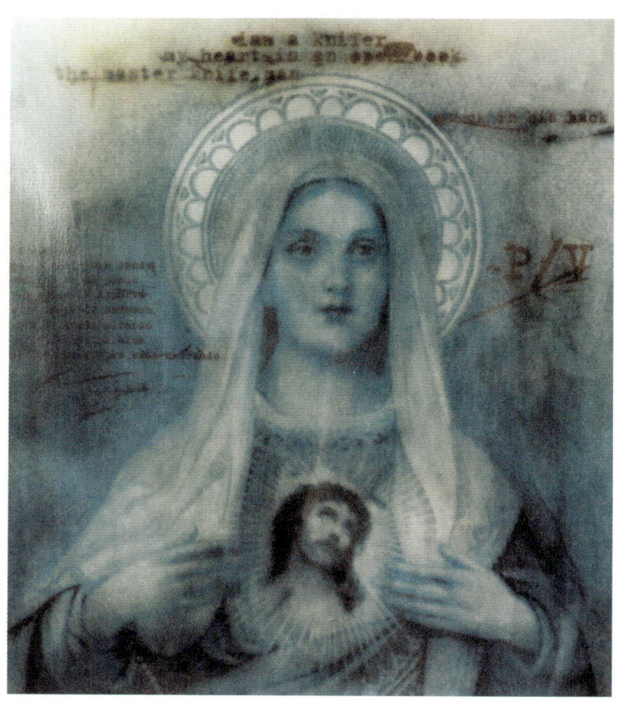

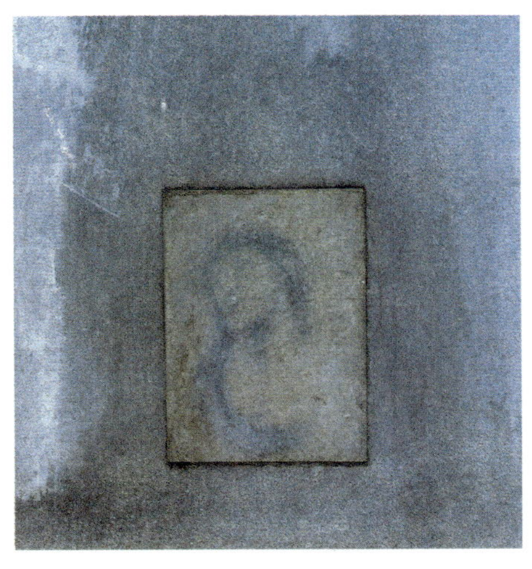

The peppers roast on the hills of *Chimayo.*
Heroin drops from the skys into vast valley.
It spits with disgrace onto the *Santuario*
where Grandfather opened the sacred land.
The Penitentes cry and the brotherhood
drops to it's knees.

The dead fingers sign and the outcome is a liar.

A liar with guns and hands of profiteering.
You see, the circle of time is controlled by the paints that created it.

i always felt my family was oddball
strange kinda violent stupid ways.
always tension spoken in spanish with the
smell of chile and lysol.
i new something wasn't right by the signs and dope.
the dope of stupidity and
machismo and angst and racism and prisons and
welfare and me and you and guns and fingers
of pure hell.

VII.

~~DARK GOATS HEARD THRU THE SHADOWS AND STREETS~~
THEY SPARE THE DETAILS OF OF THE FEET THEY'VE STEPPPED ON
TRUST NO ONE AND CONSIDER THEM ARMED
HOOFED IN BURBERRY AND POSION
~~THEY COUGH STARS TO THE SHADOW MAN~~
STARS FALL UP INTO THE BAGS OF DUST AND CHROME
ACID WASHES THE PYRAMIDS

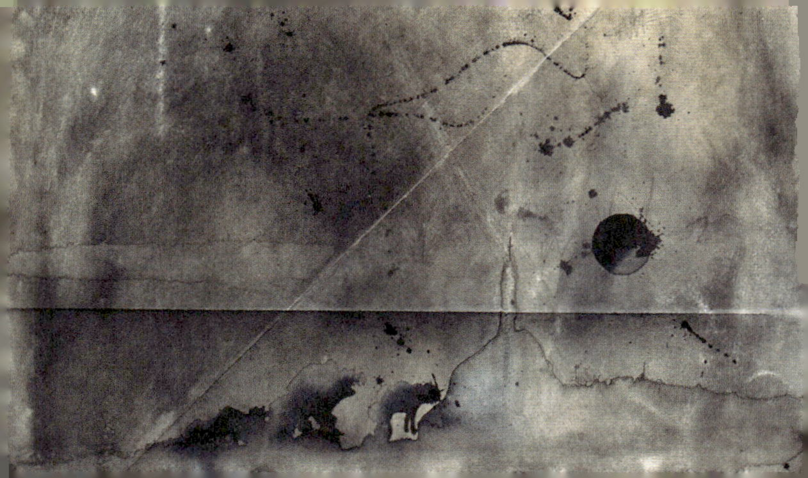

viii.

Tianguis

Mexico City, 2005

8 of 75

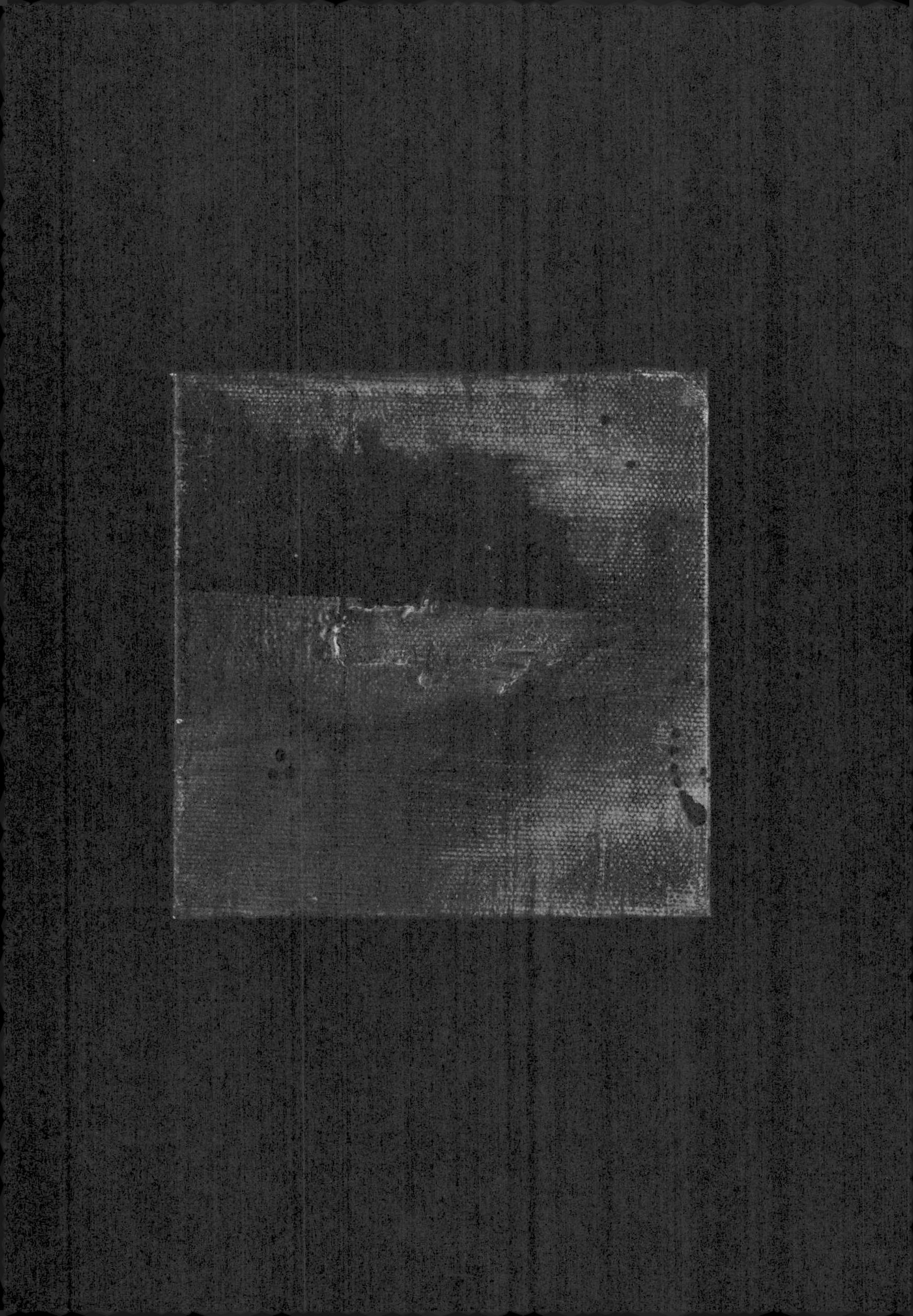

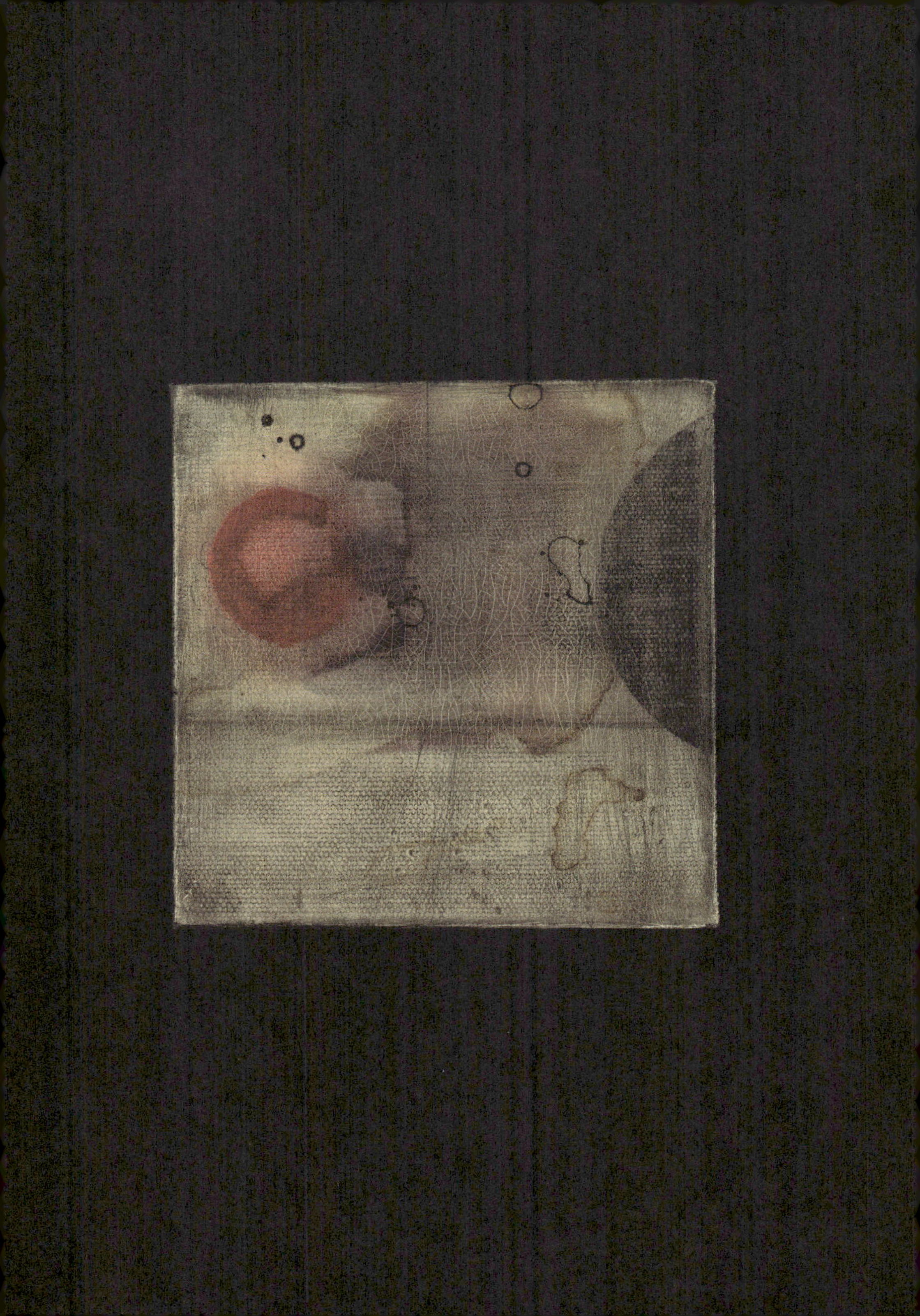

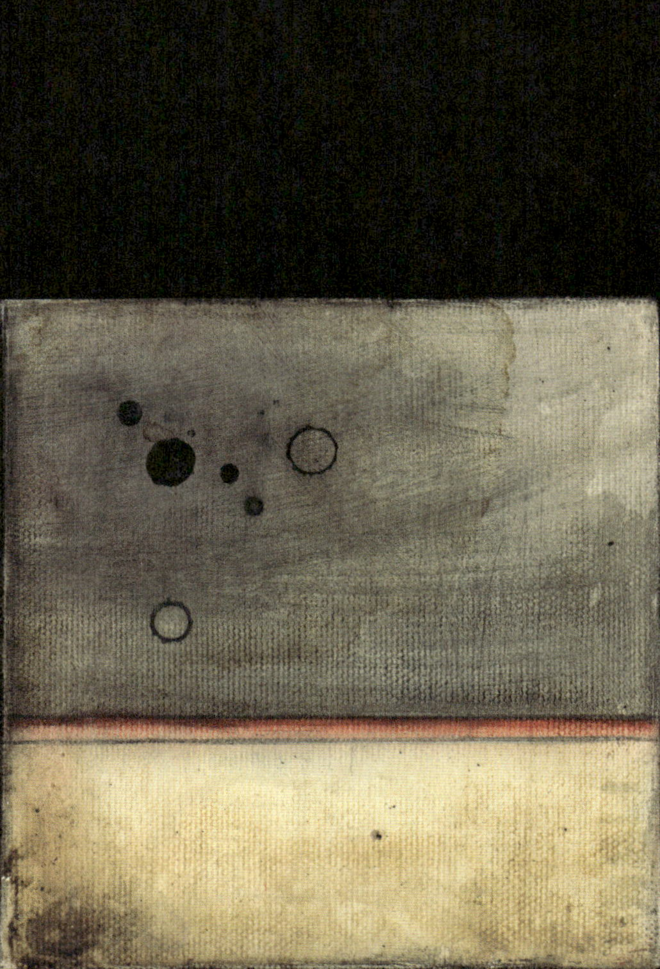

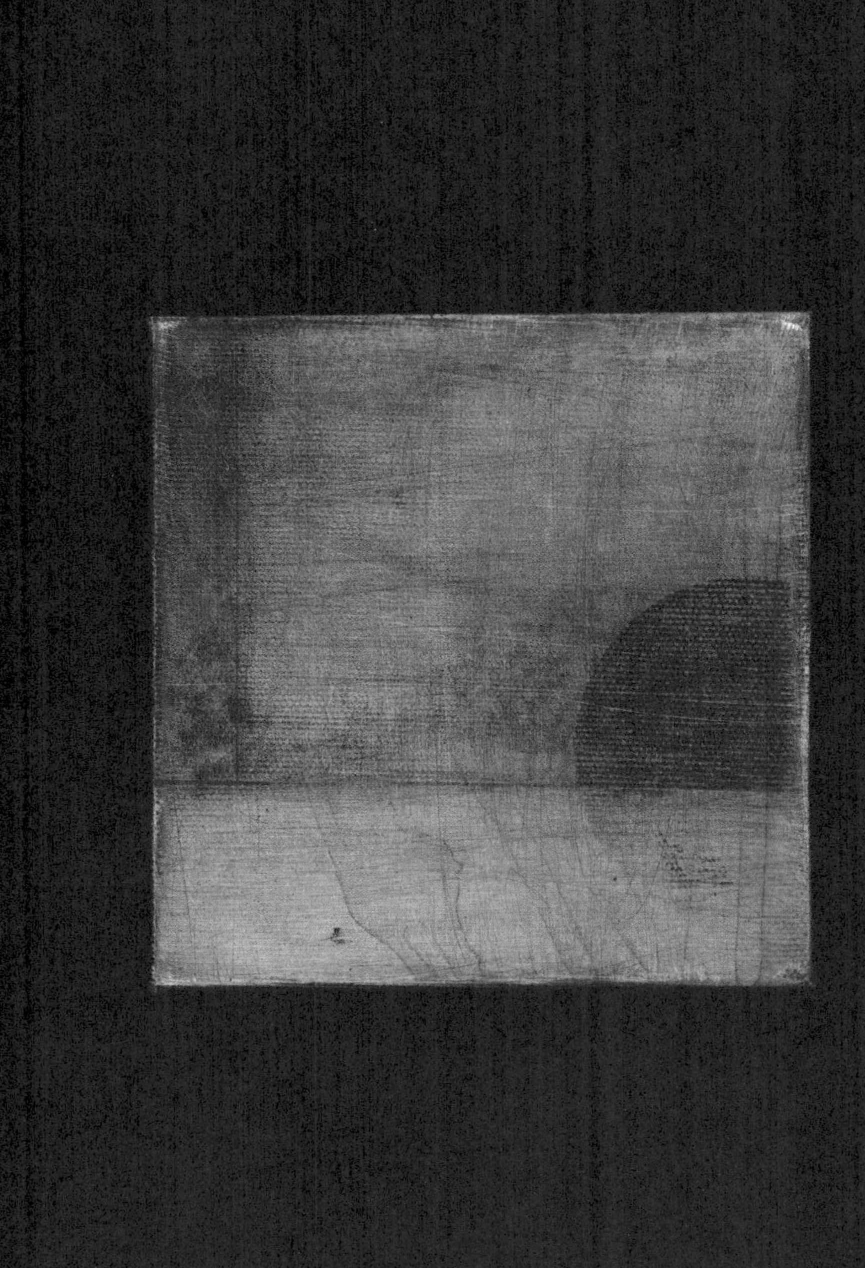

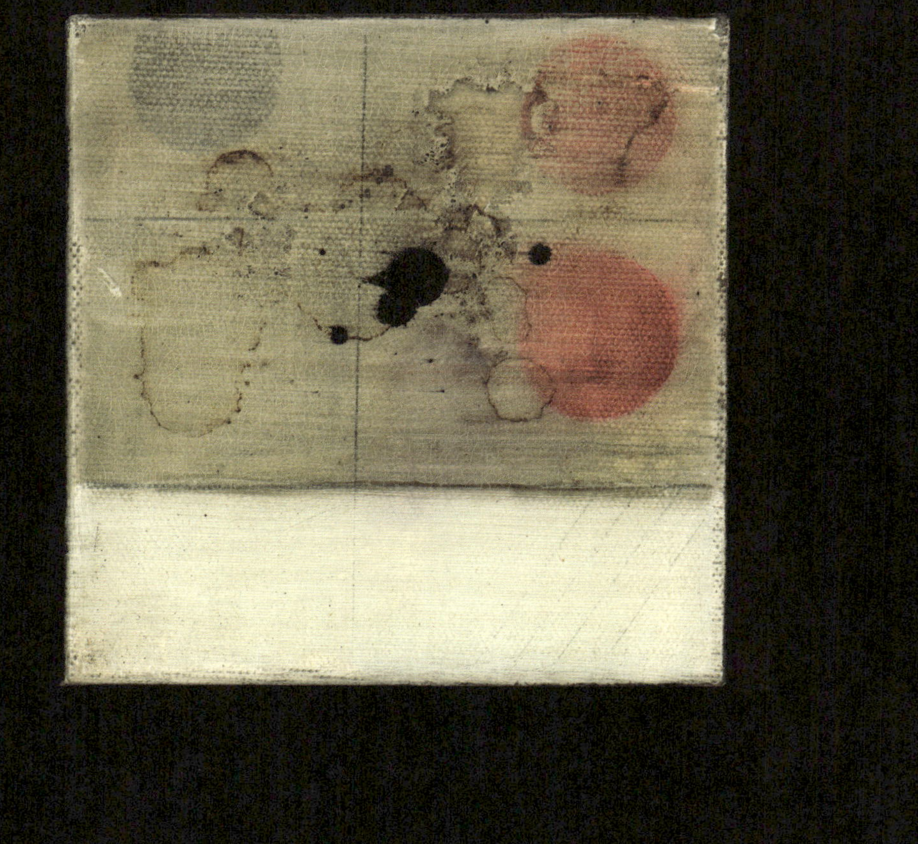

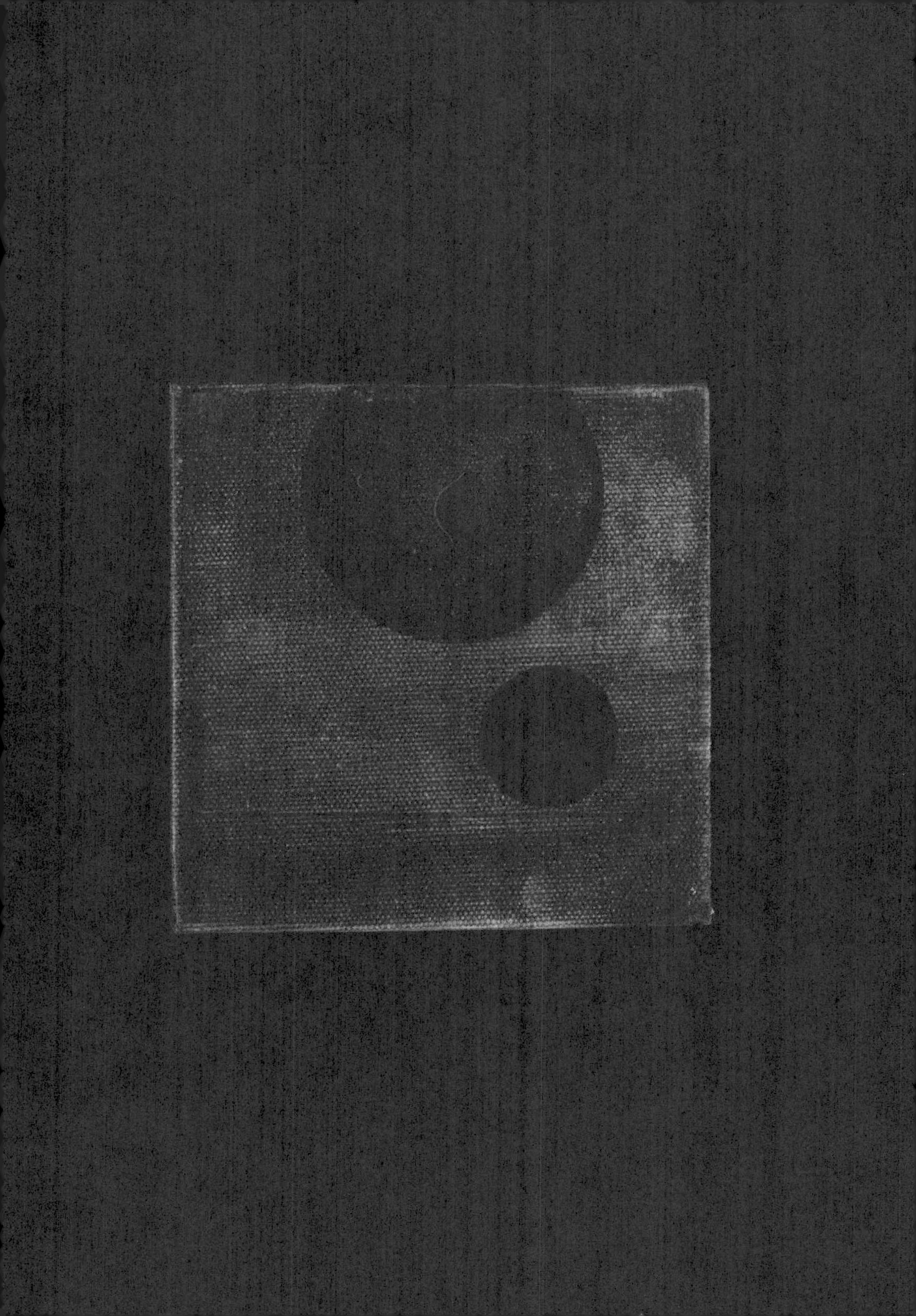

Respect & Love

Scandalous PM JC Eric D SH Rob JM SLK

JW JA JB

A CAA ELA CCA ESCA CEA N

A A

Cartoon SS (r.i.p.) Big Huero Lil Luck NE Diablo